France,
A Love Story

Edited by
Camile Cusumano

SEAL PRESS

FRANCE, A LOVE STORY:
WOMEN WRITE ABOUT THE FRENCH EXPERIENCE

Copyright © 2004 by Camille Cusumano

Published by Seal Press
An Imprint of Avalon Publishing Group, Inc.
1400 65th Street, Suite 250
AVALON Emeryville, CA 94608
publishing group incorporated

ISBN 1-58005-115-4

9 8 7 6 5 4 3 2

Cover and interior designed by Jacob Goolkasian
Printed in the United States of America by Malloy
Distributed by Publishers Group West

Contents

Pour tous ceux qui aiment la France comme la vie.

Acknowledgments

This book would not exist without the collective passion and experience of the writers within it. More than one hundred writers, from points all over the globe—Canada, France, England, Scotland, Switzerland, Japan, China, South Africa, and Burkina Faso, as well as the United States—submitted their inspiring work for this anthology and I regret that space and other editorial considerations limited their presence.

I am indebted to Leslie Miller, an editor at Seal, who gave me the nudge I needed to start moving this book idea toward birth. I'm thankful to Christina Henry de Tessan, a multitalented Seal editor (with a most pertinent Franco-American heritage) whose constant involvement in this project helped nurture it to fruition. *Mille mercis* to Elizabeth Wright, my longtime friend (and first French professor at San Francisco State many years ago) for her consultation on several things French.

Thank you, Dan, ancient friend and partner, who, as usual in the last dozen years, supported my latest literary endeavor by listening, encouraging, and most importantly believing.

Introduction

My early life was anchored in industrial New Jersey. The fifth of ten kids in a Sicilian-American family, I was shy and retiring. I read. I dreamed, especially of playing a role other than that of supportive wife and mother, which was prescribed for me and my five sisters. My family didn't travel. I escaped through books. Then, at age thirteen, I discovered French.

The French language wedged an opening in my imagination.

Speaking French was sexy. It made me sit up and use my body in startling ways. It meant a voyage to new places in my lips, tongue, nasal passage, and abdomen. My whole body resonated with the discovery of challenging vowels, consonants, and diphthongs. The new sounds ignited enough visual imagery to sustain a budding romantic: I imagined myself surrounded by a coterie of bohemian friends in Paris's Latin Quarter as we espoused bold theories on *la condition humaine*; or, I'd see myself tooling around in a Deux Chevaux on the Côte d'Azur (only English speakers would call it the Riviera).

The French language gave my persistent state of longing in the gray haze of New Jersey a *raison d'être*. My French life was a secret life, not shared even with my closest friend or sister—foreign words were uncool at that time in that place. But one evening, after I had learned all the verb tenses and the subjunctive mood, my girlfriend Mary Ellen asked me to go to a bar with her to look for her boyfriend. Feeling superior, I decided to speak only French when spoken to, filling in the gaps in my knowledge with French-sounding nonsense. Mary Ellen pretended to translate my utterances. It didn't take much to impress some uneducated barflies, but I ate up the attention and loved how I felt and sounded—even with bogus fluency.

Tu diras bien des choses chez toi (loosely: Give my regards to your family) was the first full sentence I mastered. I have never actually used this textbook idiom, but it remains an almost-sacred milestone in my rite of passage. I knew that French was my ticket to other shores.

Some years before I knew any of this, a young woman from Southern California was making a literary name for herself writing of the culinary epiphanies she experienced in France. My background could hardly have been more different from that of M. F. K. Fisher—for one thing, great feasts were not in short supply in my Sicilian-American home. I was seeking intellectual—not necessarily gastronomical—stimulation. My French-fed fantasies ranged from becoming a correspondent for the intriguingly named French magazine *Ingénue* to being a poet who presided over Parisian literary salons. Yet M. F. K. Fisher and I both found in France what was lacking for us back home.

I finally touched down on French soil after seven years of romancing the tongue. My first view of Paris—an indelible memory—was seen from a bus. My face glued to the window, I watched the City of Light solidify out of the pointillist paint of my imagination. Tableau after tableau scrolled by, with the anticipated cobblestone streets, the Arc de Triomphe, the Eiffel Tower, Notre Dame, and the Champs Elysées with its *flâneurs* and cafés bustling with interesting clientele. It seemed forever before the driver let us alight at the Place de la Concorde. I recall those spellbound days with the enchantment one feels in consummating a first love—so pure and innocent one moment, so worldly-wise the next.

That evening, I and another American woman broke from our college group to dine in a real French restaurant on chateaubriand. I wanted the pleasure of ordering a meal in my second language. That memory, of sitting in a booth as a fawning waiter responded *avec plaisir* to my every command, is bathed in warm rose lighting with hushed sounds.

A few days later, I found myself situated *en famille* in La Franqui, a small village on the Mediterranean near the border with Spain. I worked as a barmaid in the family's café and experienced the first challenges of my maiden voyage to France. I easily learned the local colloquial names of drinks—*un crème* (café with milk), *un panaché* (beer mixed with lemon soda), *un Pelforth* (French beer), *un presse* (*citron pressé*, or lemonade), and *un perroquet* (a "parrot" or beer with mint syrup). But along with a few francs, I earned the disapproval of the café's *patron* for my "loose" American ways: I wanted to mingle with the village youth after work. Our contrasting views on my social life led to my premature departure. I hitchhiked—with suitcases—slowly up the interior of *la France profonde*. Making my way back to Paris, I stretched my *sous* and relied often upon the kindness of strangers.

My first sojourn to France changed me. French studies at home and abroad threaded through the years that followed, until one day, a graduate degree in French language and literature in hand, I made my professional debut far from the shores of my dreamy youth in New Jersey. In San Francisco, I was a production assistant on a biweekly French newspaper called *Le Californien* (today it is called *Le Journal Français*).

My travels to France nurtured me through much coming of age. One summer of backpacking took me to Sète in the south, where I acquired my first French beau, Philippe Noel. He looked and dressed like Jesus Christ, and sported a blue-green crucifix tattoo on his forehead. He smoked hashish and we slept, along with an international cadre of youth, on the beach. We fetched mussels from the sea and cooked them over a bonfire.

I graduated to more sophisticated travel, and enjoyed extravagant bike tours through Provence and Brittany with the upscale Butterfield & Robinson outfit. I slept like a queen in refurbished chateaux and exquisite farmhouses, feasting on fabulous cuisine— *lapin à la moutarde* (rabbit in mustard sauce), the white asparagus of Provence, and the sugar-sweet Cavaillon melon. Tavel rosé, Côtes du Rhône, and the fabled liquid velvet of Bordeaux flowed freely. I recall a moment when, on a back road near Avignon, a man of wealth and distinction (from New Jersey!) held an edible jewel in the palm of his hand: ham and egg suspended diaphanously in a glass-smooth amber aspic. "Who but the French?" we both intoned as we marveled at the artistry of the French approach to even the most mundane of ingredients.

I knew I was not alone in my addiction to France, and have always loved to listen to others rhapsodize about their French experiences. In preparing this book, I read and enjoyed several hundred stories by women similarly "infected." I was intrigued by the pattern that emerged: women wrote not just of their love for France, but also of the pain and joy of discovering new dimensions to their very selves there. Self-discovery took many forms, from negotiating the French psyche through friendship, a love affair, or a chance encounter; to finding, as in the case of an African-American expatriate, that

"France's brand of racism is not nearly as oppressive and overwhelming as that of the United States"; to learning humility in an unheralded Arab quarter in Le Havre.

It has always been easy for foreigners to love France's food and wine, its lovely back roads, its high fashion, its august monuments. And we Americans do—we visit France more often than we do any other European country. What is more challenging is to linger past the wine and pastries and to observe and reflect as we reach across the eternal Franco-Anglo cultural divide. Each writer in this anthology has stretched herself in this context.

One writer learns her forebears' patience through the unique challenges of mushroom hunting in Gascony; another watches herself morph hilariously as she tries on stilettos. One author runs into the cutting edge of French patrimony as she helps rebuild a chateau; another surrenders to the French reverence for the tradition of Beaujolais Nouveau; and yet another bears witness to the cruel truth behind silken foie gras. Through encounters romantic, humorous, or epicurean, these travelers stumble time and again upon hidden aspects of themselves, even as they delve into the mystifying—at times maddening—culture of France.

Establishing a new persona for oneself in France is a well-documented American tradition. Famous American women, from Gertrude Stein and Natalie Clifford Barney to Josephine Baker and Janet Flanner, have left behind notable works and/or reputations forged in France.

Introduction

Some of them could have been nurtured only in France. It's not just that France, who sent Brigitte Bardot over to us in the modest American 1950s, lacks our puritanical restraint and places more emphasis on a slower, more sensual, and aesthetic way of life. It is also that France (who gave us Descartes, Voltaire, Colette, Sartre, and de Beauvoir) has a more ripened culture and that France, whose Age of Enlightenment *philosophes* influenced our own founding fathers, has long encouraged—side by side with its indisputably headstrong ways— open thinking and self expression.

The stories within this collection are diverse, yet each author writes with a passion worthy, for its magic-potion quality, of *Tristan et Iseult*. France has seduced, charmed, and uplifted generations of Americans, and, as I hope this anthology reveals, it continues to cast its incomparable spell today.

Wild Boar and
Mad Englishmen

Kay Sexton

The Ariège handles most seasons badly. Winter is long and cold, punctuated by driving rain, fog, and the sulky arrival of vast amounts of overnight snow, like meteorological trash-dumping. Spring is untidy and prone to fitful gales. Glorious summer rarely lasts more than three weeks. But autumn redeems the Ariège. Then, the scenery glows, and the Pyrenean foothills etch themselves against skies the blue of a butterfly's wing. Ducks fly overhead and mushrooms appear in the leaf litter. This is the seductive season, the one that compels foreigners to move here.

We were seduced. We found our dream home in Gudas. Gudas is our village, and we are its foreigners. When we arrived from England, we expected to have to learn French and to integrate into French culture. My mother and I had spent the previous three months reading French cookbooks, while my husband and my father practiced the names for common building tools and raw materials. We hadn't anticipated that our exoticness would be such a source of entertainment—or that speaking French would only make us boring to the community. My father, who had managed to learn only five words of French, got invited to everybody's house to drink eau de vie while I, who speak the language fluently, was left at home to deal with the agricultural assessor who was trying to understand why we wanted to turn perfectly good farmland into a campsite.

Dad got drunk—and I got angry—frequently in those first weeks. Eventually, after a mammoth tussle with officialdom that included flying down a "specialist in tourism" from Paris, we received permission to build a campsite in our meadows and to turn three farm buildings into vacation cottages, or *gîtes*. And my father recovered from a four-day hangover swearing he would never look at cherry liqueur again. To my great delight, my father's attempt to purchase antifreeze for his truck entered local legend. His mime of heavy snowfall and a dead engine enchanted our garage owner, who was also the mayor and who was still telling the story six years later when he visited the school to give prizes to the first-year students. I know because my son came home to tell me that when Granddad arrived in Gudas, he performed a snowman dance and the mayor laughed so much he nearly wet his pants. Humor, like much else in the Ariège, must be robust to survive.

Foreigners have to be robust, too.

One of the first lessons we learned when we moved here is that there is no such thing as a mushroom. *Champignon* is a word describing a gray-beige color—not food. There are chanterelles, *girolles, boletes, cèpes,* and *têtes-de-nègre,* but no mushrooms.

Mushrooms are what effete Parisians eat. Like most agricultural communities, the Ariègeois will not eat what they cannot name with precision. *Champignon* is a wholly unacceptable term, *cèpe* is barely satisfactory, *cèpe de Pamiers* is better, *cèpe d'entre Pamiers Varilhes* is better still, and *cèpe de bois Perrouty, Varilhes Commune,* is best. It means *cèpe* harvested from the woodland that is part of the field called Perrouty in the commune of Varilhes. Very best of all, though, is *cèpe moi-même*—the *cèpe* I found myself.

The *cèpe* (or *bolete* or chanterelle) *moi-même* is the culinary holy grail of every Ariègeois. It brings them home from all over Europe every autumn weekend. The fugitive Ariègeois summer restores few of its sons and daughters, but mushroom season returns far-flung offspring to the family home—or more accurately, to the family woodlands.

From September to early November, the same scenes are enacted across the Ariège. Airbeds are inflated, camp beds are rescued from cellars and beaten to remove spiders, and pillows on sofas and sleeping bags on chaises longues are arranged to provide resting places for arriving relatives and their friends. Each mushroom insists on appearing at its own special time, like a diva of uncertain temperament. This means the makeshift beds have rotating shifts.

Chanterelle hunters leave the house at dawn. So, the night before a chanterelle hunt, those who favor this buttery, pumpkin-colored fungus sleep downstairs in the living rooms. This leaves the bedrooms free for the *cèpe* hunters, who may set out anytime between 10 A.M. and 2 P.M., depending on whether they hunt *cèpe* for their own lunch (10 A.M. start) or to sell at tomorrow's weekly village market (2 P.M. start). The later you cut your fungus feast, the fresher it will look next day, but beware! If you leave home at 2 P.M., you may find yourself still hunting *cèpe* at 6:30 P.M., in the dark, with only a flashlight and a fed-up dog for company—and the dog would go home if it dared.

That's how addictive mushroom hunting becomes. Whether you call it *boletus*, *cèpe de Bordeaux*, or *tête-de-nègre* (politically incorrect, but not a single French neighbor knows *boletus aureus* by any other name than "head-of-a-black-man") this fungus is the ultimate, the 24-carat, the subject of superlatives. *Cèpes* appear only when the weather is perfect. Such precise circumstances are required to produce them that a whole folklore exists around their uncertain emergence. It's true that they grow only where pigs travel, so unless the *sanglier*—wild boar—cross your land, you will not be rewarded with bowling-ball-sized fungi that taste of smoked bacon but have a texture all their own, perhaps best described as being like truffle-flavored oysters. That taste, the villagers claim, is produced, alchemically, from the dung left by the pigs.

Sanglier roam my family's land, because we are designated *chasse interdit*. This means that hunters are banned from our property. The truth, like all truths here, is more complicated. Take, for example, the day I was walking our fences checking for damage by wild boar, whose bloody-minded habits include digging up fence posts instead of walking around them. I had collapsed at the top of la Garosse, a field so steep we haul its new fence posts up on ropes because we can't carry them and walk upright. I suddenly found myself with an audience of three hunters and seven dogs.

"*Plouh*," I said to them. *Plouh* is an Ariègeois expression of disgust or exasperation. It starts in the lower gut and ends with an explosive snort through the nostrils, and is deeply insulting. "Our land is *chasse interdit*, and we are a tourist site, which means you cannot enter our boundaries with guns or unleashed dogs—there are signs posted everywhere," I told them.

"*Eh bien*," said the leading hunter, "well, we were following Nino and as you well know, Nino can't read French." It's true: Nino not only cannot read French, he cannot even *speak* it. He uses the local dialect, which is a variant of Langue d'Oc. Nino is seventy-eight years old and walks eight miles a day with the *brebis* from Barre, our local cheese-makers. *Brebis* are free-range sheep—they eat as they walk, and this gives them a different kind of milk, less fatty and more robust. It makes wonderful hard cheese that we eat greedily whenever we can get our hands on it; unfortunately, most of the Barre cheese is sold right out from under our noses to rich Parisians.

Right then, Nino was helpfully testing the fence posts, trying to rock them back and forth in their sockets. He looked relaxed, as though the hike to the top of la Garosse were a stroll across a driving range. I was pleased to see the other hunters were panting as much as I.

"*Plouh!*" said Nino. Then, in lieu of a shared language, he used energetic mime to show me that one post was shaky and would bring down the entire fence in the next snowstorm. He took the mallet and wooden wedges from me and smartly banged wedges into two sides of the post, then handed me back the mallet. The post was immovable. So were Nino and the hunters. I offered grudging thanks and headed back down "my" mountain. Nino and his companions ostentatiously moved to the other side of our boundary fence and watched me go. As soon as I was out of sight they would be back on our land, hunting the *sanglier* that had loosened the fence post. There was nothing I could do to stop them. During my journey back down, my head was filled with vicious imaginary scenes in which they roused a hibernating bear and got mauled. The rare Pyrenean bears have never come down from the mountains onto our land, but I could dream.

Then there was Monsieur Bonnard, who owned an eighth of an acre of land on one side of our access road. He owned it because it gave him shooting rights in Gudas. The owner before us, in moments of financial need, had sold several such plots. We'd bought them all back—all except the Bonnard plot. He refused to sell. He refused to exchange that land for other land, away from the road; he insisted that his minuscule plot was perfect for his needs.

So, every year, we drive past M. Bonnard sitting on a camp stool, often under an umbrella, with his gun on his knee. He is "waiting for something to shoot." Right in the middle of our hunt-banned land waits a man on his own tiny patch of hunting territory with a gun and the desire to perform carnage on songbirds, vermin, and game. The sight of him upsets our foreign visitors, who come here to watch the wildlife, especially the boar, polecats, and eagles. M. Bonnard never actually shoots anything on our land. He knows that if he did, we would haul him down to the *mairie* and have his *permis de chasse* revoked. But this one day's "hunting" on our land qualifies him to enter the Gudas Hunts, in which drivers and beaters hit the undergrowth with sticks and yell to force all walking or flying game into the path of the guns. This brings regular kills of substantial amounts of game. For a share of those boar and deer carcasses, he sits on his patch of land inside our hunting-prohibited boundaries.

In the spirit of community, we tolerate him. The twin law codes of hunting and tourism form an uneasy alliance, and M. Bonnard's putative shooting rights on our land are an example of the complexity that the Ariègeois love. Two years ago, M. Bonnard (his first name is Francis-Xavier, but we have never been invited to use it) introduced us to his grandson, Xavier-Luc. Xavier-Luc will inherit the duty of sitting on his land inside our land once a year, being stared at by the tourists who hire our *gîtes* or set up campers in our fields. In this way he will keep alive the local tradition of intransigence, and—almost despite myself—I applaud him for it.

Because we have *sanglier* in our woods, we also have *cèpes*. And that is where the cultural chasm yawns open.

My father believes that a man's land is sacrosanct, and that good fences make good neighbors. Every Ariègeois also believes both those things to be true—that is, unless one's neighbor has something like cherries, or wild strawberries, or chestnuts or walnuts or *cèpes*, at which point the rules change. If you have a wild crop and you don't appear to be harvesting it, or it is obvious that you can't use all of it yourself, or if your land was once owned by a distant cousin of theirs, then average Ariègeois feel they have a sacred duty to uphold the proverb "Waste not, want not" by helping you out with the harvesting, storage, and consumption of that produce.

Between September and November my mother, my husband, and I hear regular bellows from the woodlands that surround our house: "What the hell do you think you're doing? Did I give you permission to come here and scavenge in my woods? No, I did not! Kay, get down here now, I've caught some more of them! What have you got in the basket? Right, those are my *cèpes*, thank you very much, I'll have those back for a start! Kay, get down here, there's more of these thieving swine all over the wood! Come and give them hell!"

My father still hasn't mastered the French language. Like Nino, he relies on powerful pantomime to convey his feelings, and no mushroom hunter who has confronted his stick-waving, roaring, red-faced fury has failed to get the message. The first year I ran down every time to explain politely to the mushroom marauder that we did indeed know what *cèpes* were, that we did eat them when we found them and that yes, we did know that these woods were ours, so would they please leave?

I did this to save my father's heart, which seemed likely to explode in fury at every trespass he discovered. The trespassers were incredulous. No other "*étranger*" ate mushrooms; surely we were worried about being poisoned? Well, no, actually. We are pretty confident about the mushrooms we eat and no one has been ill yet. But surely we did strange things to them, things that destroyed the taste and made a mockery of the wonderful French tradition of eating anything that isn't nailed down or three months dead? Well, no, actually. We put chanterelles in soup and omelettes. We slice our *cèpes* and fry them in butter. Just like everyone else here. "*Eh bien,*" the trespasser would concede, handing over the mushrooms, "*bon appétit!*"

The second year, I just yelled from wherever I happened to be that we were not as stupid as we looked, and if the unwelcome visitors didn't leave immediately, and mushroomless, I would call city hall and subject them to an embarrassing public scolding. My father's heart seemed to hold up pretty well under this rather distant threat process, so I spent the third short summer teaching my father to say "*Plouh! Donnez-les moi!*" This simple message, repeated at full volume, rang through our third autumn, scaring fledgling birds from the trees and causing guiltless campers to jump out of their skins. I'm sure it's good for my father to speak for himself in these matters. He gets to meet many of our neighbors and engage with them in their own tongue, and it has certainly improved his French accent.

The rest of my family still see these incursions onto our land as larcenous. Back home, when we wanted to visit neighbors, we would use the main drive, but villagers here arrive from all directions: over the top of la Garosse (with pockets stuffed with sloes), from Perrouty (empty-handed but ready to harvest the *cèpes* or cherries they earmarked on their inward journey), or from Source d'Eau, the marshy field that runs along the front of our property and produces flag iris and bulrushes that adorn many a vase in our village. Back home, we'd call this theft. Here it's called nothing—it's just the law of the land. If your neighbor is too busy, lazy, or stupid to harvest nature's products, you just help yourself. Then, when the time is right, you repay whatever benefit you've gained. The fence posts at la Garosse will never be loose again, as long as Nino walks our land with the *brebis*. His employers at Barre, the master cheesemakers Geneviève and Pierre, will drop in a wheel of good *brebis* cheese around November, to thank us for the grazing rights we "give" them.

We are expected to understand the economics of life in rural France. This means we must recognize that the chanterelles and cherries Nino takes back are part of the bargain we keep with Barre. What all our neighbors know is that if we didn't have the Barre sheep, we'd have to mow our front fields and that would cost us time, labor, and mower maintenance costs. Then we'd need to bale the meadow grass, and find a buyer for it. It's a complex equation that we will probably never master in full. I can see only the vague outlines of it, and my parents can't see it at all. Barre sheep have been grazing our land since World War II. We are not the originators of this exchange, any more than Geneviève and Pierre are; we are just the current cogs in a beautifully oiled machine that keeps the Ariège alive—farming mountain land is hard work, and we all have to accept our share of interdependence if it's to succeed.

We are already indebted to our neighbors beyond any repayment. For two years while our property lay ownerless—the two years before we bought it—they walked our land. They cleared brambles from our mailbox. They checked our water source each spring and patched cracks in our clay irrigation pipe. They grazed their animals on the land and kept the meadows in sweet grass instead of allowing them to become rank, weedy plains. They pulled down fallen trees and cut them for firewood, preserving our electricity cables and the rest of our woodlands from domino-like falls.

They took the wood, of course, for their own log piles. That's how it works here, and before we can call ourselves Ariègeois, we must learn this wondrous system of "What's yours is mine as long as I keep it in good shape and you don't get to it first."

This year, I aim to persuade my family to launch preemptive strikes against our neighbors—the first *cèpe* day of autumn will find us ranging far and wide with our baskets and knives. Who knows? Perhaps the *cèpe moi-même* will taste all the richer if we find it on somebody else's land.

The Mother of Vinegar

Margaret Judge

When one thinks of a gift from Paris, the kinds of things that come to mind are a bottle of perfume, a purse of supple leather, a colorful silk scarf with a designer's signature in the corner. But the gift from Paris that I cherish most wasn't purchased in a boutique on the Champs Elysées or from a showcase window of the high priests of French glamour on rue du Faubourg Saint-Honoré.

My husband and I arrived in Paris on Bastille Day and went directly to the apartment that would be our home for two months while George worked on a National Science Foundation project from an office at INSEE, the French Economic Institute. The apartment, located on the top floor of a three-story building at 51 rue Cardinet, belonged to Madame Claude, who met us there in order to acquaint us with its features before going to her second home in the south of France.

Madame Claude was older than I expected, and meeting her was like finding a grandmother I didn't know I had. She wore a stylish silk dress; her soft white hair was pulled behind her ears and fastened in a chignon at the nape of her neck. A wide smile and bright eyes with thin, arched eyebrows gave her face a look of constant surprise.

"Come, come, let me show you around," she said, her English words softened by a French accent. Then, linking her arm with mine, she walked with me down the wide hallway.

Entering the living room was like stepping into a Renaissance painting. The walls were covered with white paneling trimmed in gold, and elegant antique furniture, upholstered in rose-colored velvet, gave a luxurious feel to the room. Long shelves of books in both French and English and a collection of paintings and sculptures were evidence of Madame Claude's interest in literature and art.

The walls and ceiling of the bedroom we were to sleep in were covered in rich blue silk taffeta. Light from delicate crystal wall sconces twinkled in the mirrored doors of an antique armoire that served as a closet. Swagged drapes of the shiny blue fabric surrounded the bed, giving it the look of a giant gift-wrapped package.

The small kitchen was plain compared with the other rooms in the apartment. But when I saw the shiny copper pans hanging from hooks above the stove, the heavy crock of garlic and shallots sitting on the counter, and fresh herbs growing in flowerpots on the sill of the open window, I fell in love with it. Madame Claude showed us how to light the gas stove, use the coffee grinder, dispose of the garbage, and find the fuse box, all things we needed to know. Then she took a large glass jar from a kitchen cabinet.

"You'll need to feed the vinegar," she said.

Feed the vinegar? I'd taken care of pets and tended house plants for other people before, but I knew nothing about the care and feeding of vinegar.

Holding the jar up to the light, Madame Claude pointed to a dark red shape that looked like a chunk of beef liver lurking at the bottom.

"That is the 'mother' of vinegar that causes wine to ferment and turn to vinegar. This 'mother' has been handed down in my family, and I do hope you'll nurture it while I'm away," she said, looking at me and nodding her head for emphasis. "Keep the jar inside the cabinet, away from the light. Make sure the cap is not airtight so the 'mother' can breathe, and don't forget to feed it some red wine each day."

After the apartment tour, Madame Claude urged us to go to the Bastille Day parade while she cooked dinner for us. Tired from our overnight flight from the United States, we were reluctant to leave the comfortable apartment. However, the military parade along the Champs Elysées was exciting, and being part of the celebration was an appropriate welcome for our French sojourn. While we were out, we stopped in a wine shop and, after much discussion and advice from the wine merchant, bought a bottle of Côtes du Rhone for dinner and a bottle of champagne to celebrate my first evening in Paris.

It was late but still light out when we returned and opened the apartment door to the rich aroma of simmering shallots, mushrooms, and herbs. The table was set and the dinner was cooked. But before we could eat, Madame Claude insisted on teaching me how to make a French vinaigrette using her own wine vinegar.

In the bottom of a large salad bowl, she combined some of the vinegar with fresh lemon juice, Dijon mustard, a pinch of salt, and freshly ground black pepper. She gradually added olive oil, whisking until the dressing thickened slightly, then added the fresh salad greens and tossed it all together. The dinner of veal and fresh vegetables was delectable and the salad, made with the pungent, earthy vinaigrette and served after the main course, was excellent.

Madame Claude left early the next morning, and soon our days in Paris began to pass quickly. George went to INSEE every weekday and I set off each morning with my string bag to gather the ingredients for the dinners I prepared at night. I located the *boulangerie* that sold the flakiest croissants and the baguettes with the crispest crust. I learned I would get the best cut of veal if I dropped some francs into the breast pocket of the butcher's starched white coat. I found the produce vendor was patient with my fractured French, and even pleased that I tried to use the language, and picked out the firmest tomatoes and the juiciest peaches for me. I made a friend of the wine merchant and bought a variety of delicious wines for drinking, for cooking, and for sharing with the vinegar mother.

Two afternoons a week I went to La Varenne Cooking School and watched a chef demonstrate cooking methods as he prepared classic French dishes: *boeuf bourguignon*, cassoulet, crepes, tapenade. For the grand finale, he would make chocolate éclairs, a fruit-filled tart, or a feather-light sponge cake. At the end of each session, the students were given the recipes and a taste of the food.

Other days, I explored Paris by Metro and on foot. Some of my favorite places were the Cluny Museum, where I spent hours admiring the Unicorn tapestries; Sainte-Chapelle, where I returned many times to marvel at the Gothic architecture and the beautiful stained-glass windows; and Parc Monceau, where I sat in the sunshine and enjoyed watching the well-dressed children at play.

In the evenings we ate fluffy omelettes, rich soup, ratatouille, or veal escalopes that I prepared and served with crusty bread and salad made with Madame Claude's vinegar. Each time I took vinegar from the jar, I replaced it with an equal amount of wine, and the vinegar, bolstered by the robust and complex flavors of the French red wines, remained the consistently tart and flavorful product it had been for years.

I became curious about this shadowy mother with the miraculous power to change wine into vinegar. I stared at the gelatinous, slippery mass at the bottom of the jar, and wondered what it was made of and if it was a living organism. I asked several people about the mother, but what it was and how it worked remained a mystery until I finally found an explanation in one of Madame Claude's cookbooks.

The mother of vinegar is a jellylike formation of bacteria and yeast cells that develop spontaneously in wine that is left uncorked in a warm, dark place. In about a month, the combination of oxygen and alcohol in the wine starts a fermentation process and the mother develops. Once it is formed, it fosters the production of acetic acid, the key ingredient in vinegar. Wine that is added to the mother will sour and become vinegar. A well-fed mother will grow and ensure a supply of flavorful vinegar for many years.

By our last evening at 51 rue Cardinet, I felt well acquainted with "mother's eating habits" and confident of my skill to nurture her. Madame Claude returned and George and I prepared a dinner for her: sole *en croûte*, a recipe I had learned at La Varenne, and Bibb lettuce salad tossed with a perfect vinaigrette.

The next morning while I was packing, Madame Claude broke off a piece of the mother as a farewell gift for me. I was pleased with my gift, truly a living piece of my French experience. But I worried about taking it on the airplane. I wondered if my luggage would smell of vinegar, and if the agricultural inspectors would allow me to take her into the United States.

Madame Claude and I exchanged light kisses on both cheeks as we said goodbye. I felt sad that my time in Paris was ending. I wondered when I would return and if I would see Madame Claude again.

The "mother" survived the flight home and the scrutiny of the agricultural inspectors. She flourished in my American kitchen, and French vinaigrette became my specialty. With time, the mother grew large enough for me to share it with friends, which linked us all in a new way.

I saw Madame Claude again—each time my husband and I returned to Paris and rented her apartment. Our friendship grew, and one summer we visited her in her summer home, near Carcassonne, a lovely old stone building that had once been a mill.

Now, someone else owns the apartment at 51 rue Cardinet and Madame Claude is no longer living, but the gift she gave to me—and by extension to others—still goes on giving.

Long Ago in France

M. F. K. Fisher

The first night in the new quarters, after we had moved and arranged about having Al's trunks of books sent from the station, I looked up the word *anniversary* in my dictionary and told Madame that it was our first one. "Impossible," she shouted, glaring at me and then roaring with laughter when I said, "Three weeks, not even a month. We would like to go to a nice restaurant to celebrate," I said.

She ripped a piece of paper off a package on the wine-stained tablecloth, scrawled on it with a pencil stub she always seemed to have somewhere about her, and said, "Here . . . you know where the Ducal Palace is? The place d'Armes: You will see a sign there, the Three Pheasants. Give this to Monsieur Racouchot."

And she laughed again, as if I were amusing in an imbecilic way. I didn't mind.

We changed our clothes in the unfamiliar rooms. The lights were on wires with weighted pulleys, so that by sliding them up or down you could adjust their distance from the ceiling, and there was a kind of chain running through the socket of each one, which regulated the power of the light. There were fluted glass shades like pie pans, with squares of brown and purple sateen over them, weighted at each corner with a glass bead. The shadows in the unfamiliar corners, and on our faces, were dreadful in those mauve and mustard chambers.

But we felt beautiful. We put on our best clothes, and tiptoed down the wide stone stairs and past the lighted dining room, with a great key in Al's pocket and our hearts pounding . . . our first real meal alone together in a restaurant in France.

First we went up the rue Chabot-Charny to the Café de Paris, by the theater. It was Al's first love, and a faithful one. He worked there almost every day we lived in Dijon, and grew to know its waiters, the prostitutes who had their morning cards-and-coffee there, its regular patrons, and the rolling population of stock-actors and singers, who were playing at the theater across the street. It was warm in winter, and as cool and fresh as any provincial café could be in the summer. I liked it as soon as I walked shyly into it, that first night.

We were very ignorant about French *apéritifs*, so Al read from a sign above the cash desk when the waiter came, and said, "The Cocktail Montana, please." The waiter looked delighted, and dashed to the bar. After quite a while he brought a large tumbler, rimmed with white sugar, and filled with a golden-pink liquid. There were two straws stuck artfully on the frosted glass, one on Al's side and one on mine.

Al was a little embarrassed that he had not ordered clearly for both of us, but as it turned out, anything else would have been a disaster: The Cocktail Montana whipped up by the Café de Paris was one of the biggest, strongest, loudest drinks I ever drank.

We learned later that a traveling cowboy, stranded from a small Yankee circus, offered to teach its priceless secret to the café owner for free beer, promising him that Americans for miles around would flock to buy it . . . at nine francs a throw, instead of the one franc fifty ordinary drinks cost there. Of course, there were no Americans to flock; the few who stopped in Dijon sipped reverently of rare wines at the Three Pheasants or the Cloche, or good wines in any café, and would have shuddered with aesthetic and academic horror at such a concoction as we took turns drinking that night.

We enjoyed it immensely (we even had it once or twice again in the next three years, in a kind of sentimental loyalty), and walked on toward the Ducal Palace feeling happier than before.

We saw the big gold letters, Aux Trois Faisans, above a dim little café. It looked far from promising, but we went in, and showed Madame Ollangnier's scribbled note to the man behind the bar. He laughed, looked curiously at us, and took Al by the arm, as if we were deaf and dumb. He led us solicitously out into the great semicircular *place*, and through an arch next to the café with two bay trees in tubs on either side. We were in a bare beautiful courtyard. A round light burned over a doorway.

The man laughed again, gave us each a silent little push toward the light, and disappeared. We never saw him again, but I remember how pleased he seemed to be, to leave his own café for a few minutes and direct such obviously bemazed innocents upstairs to Racouchot's. Probably it had never occurred to him, a good Burgundian, that anyone in the world did not know exactly how to come from any part of it straight to the famous door.

The first meal we had was a shy stupid one, but even if we had never gone back and never learned gradually how to order food and wine, it would still be among the important ones in my life.

We were really very timid that first time, but soon it all would become familiar to us. The noisy dark staircase and the big glass case with dead fish and lobsters and mushrooms and grapes piled on the ice no longer seemed strange to us. And after the first summer I never could pass the water closets with their swinging doors without remembering my mother's consternation when she had first entered them and found them full of men all chatting, easing themselves, and belching appreciatively. Her face puckered in an effort to look broad-minded.

The long hall past the kitchens and small private dining rooms and Racouchot's office, and the two dining rooms for the *pensionnaires*, then the dining room . . . I grew to know them as well as I know my own house now.

The glass door to Monsieur Racouchot's small and incredibly disordered office was usually closed, but we knew that it was often filled with the conglomerate cooking odors of a good meal being served to him and one or two of his cooks in their tall white bonnets.

The only regular *pensionnaires* we knew were Monsieur Venot, the town bookseller, from his shop on the corner two streets down on the place d'Armes, and one of the *Lycée* teachers, Jean Matrouchot.

As for the private dining rooms across the hall from the main room, we seldom saw them except in passing. They were usually occupied by groups of wine men or famous politicians visiting the Mayor, Gaston Gérard. Once or twice we engaged one to entertain some of Al's friends from Princeton, who had come down from Balliol College in Oxford, people like William Mode Spackman and his wife Maryanne and her sister Dorothea, who had once been engaged to Al. We ordered especially good wines for them and I remember being much impressed when one of their guests grandly reordered a bottle of the best wine we had yet dared offer to anyone, a 1919 Gevrey-Chambertin of formidable reputation and equal price. It seemed almost sacrilegious to me that anyone could be so nonchalant about ordering so expensive a wine. I almost forgot their pitying acceptance of our strange *toilette* in our apartment on the rue du Petit-Potet, and I was glad to send them off filled with not only Racouchot's fabulous wines but with his remarkable cuisine.

This long approach to the heart of the restaurant, the main dining room, was unlike any we had ever known. Always before we had stepped almost from the street to a table, and taken it for granted that somewhere, discreetly hidden and silenced, were kitchen and offices and storage rooms. Here it was reversed, so that by the time we came to the little square dining room, the *raison d'être* of all this light and bustle and steam and planning, its quiet plainness was almost an anticlimax.

There were either nine or eleven tables in it, to hold four people, and one round one in the corner for six or eight. There were a couple of large misty oil paintings, the kind that nobody needs to look at, of autumn or perhaps spring landscapes. And there were three large mirrors.

The one at the end of the room, facing the door, had a couple of little signs on it, one recommending some kind of cocktail which we never ordered and never saw anyone else drink either, and the other giving the price by carafe and half-carafe of the red and white *vins de maison*. As far as I know, we were the only people who ever ordered that: Racouchot was so famous for his Burgundian cellar that everyone who came there knew just what fabulous wine to command, even if it meant saving for weeks beforehand. We did not yet know enough.

We went into the room shyly, and by luck got the fourth table, in a corner at the far end, and the services of a small bright-eyed man with his thinning hair waxed into a rococo curlicue on his forehead.

His name was Charles, we found out later, and we knew him for a long time and learned a great deal from him. That first night he was more than kind to us, but it was obvious that there was little he could do except see that we were fed without feeling too ignorant. His tact was great, and touching. He put the big menus in our hands and pointed out two plans for us, one at twenty-two francs and the other, the *diner de luxe au prix fixe*, at twenty-five.

We took the latter, of course, although the other was fantastic enough . . . a series of blurred legendary words: *pâte truffé Charles le*

Témpéraire, poulet en cocotte aux Trois Faisons, civet à la mode bour-guignonne . . . and in eight or nine courses. . . .

We were lost, naturally, but not particularly worried. The room was so intimate and yet so reassuringly impersonal, and the people were so delightfully absorbed in themselves and their plates, and the waiter was so nice.

He came back. Now I knew him well enough to be sure that he liked us and did not want to embarrass us, so instead of presenting us with the incredible wine book, he said, "I think that Monsieur will enjoy trying, for tonight, a carafe of our own red. It is simple, but very interesting. And may I suggest a half-carafe of the white for an appetizer? Monsieur will agree with me that it is not bad at all with the first courses. . . ."

That was the only time Charles ever did that, but I have always blessed him for it. One of the great wines, which I have watched other people order there through snobbism or timidity when they knew as little as we did, would have been utterly wasted on us. Charles started us out right, and through the months watched us with his certain deft guidance learn to know what wine we wanted, and why.

That first night, as I think back on it, was amazing. The only reason we survived it was our youth . . . and perhaps the old saw that what you don't know won't hurt you. We drank, besides the astounding Cocktail Montana, almost two liters of wine, and then coffee, and then a little sweet liqueur whose name we had learned, something like Grand Marnier or Cointreau. And we ate the biggest, as well as the most exciting, meal that either of us had ever had.

As I remember, it was not difficult to keep on, to feel a steady avid curiosity. Everything that was brought to the table was so new, so wonderfully cooked, that what might have been with sated palates a gluttonous orgy was, for our ignorance, a constant refreshment. I know that never since have I eaten so much. Even the thought of a *prix-fixe* meal, in France or anywhere, makes me shudder now. But that night the kind ghosts of Lucullus and Brillat-Savarin as well as Rabelais and a hundred others stepped in to ease our adventurous bellies, and soothe our tongues. We were immune, safe in a charmed gastronomical circle.

We learned fast, and never again risked such surfeit . . . but that night it was all right.

I don't know now what we ate, but it was the sort of rich winy spiced cuisine that is typical of Burgundy, with many dark sauces and gamey meats and ending, I can guess, with a *soufflé* of kirsch and *glacé* fruits, or some such airy trifle.

We ate slowly and happily, watched over by little Charles, and the wine kept things from being gross and heavy inside us.

When we finally went home, to unlock the little door for the first time and go up the zigzag stairs to our own rooms, we wove a bit perhaps. But we felt as if we had seen the far shores of another world. We were drunk with the land breeze that blew from it, and the sure knowledge that it lay waiting for us.

We went back often to The Three Pheasants during the next three years, and in 1954, when I returned to the city for the Foire Gastronomique, I found that Racouchot had died and that his famous restaurant had been combined with the restaurant below it on the place d'Armes, the Pré aux Clercs. This was a good move, I am sure, but it never had the magic for me of the old restaurant upstairs.

The Fisher Baron's Secret

Diane LeBow

I found Paris especially difficult to leave that morning. Familiar buildings and monuments glistened with fresh snow that had fallen during the night. Teary-eyed, I almost fell as I skidded over the medieval cobblestones of my Marais apartment courtyard for the last time. The cabby studied me in his rearview mirror.

"Why are you leaving Paris?"

"Because I must return to my job and home in San Francisco."

"Tsk tsk"—the ultimate French negation—and a slow-motion shake of his head registered the cab driver's displeasure.

"What matters in life is that you make love with someone you care about on Sunday morning and walk out with them on Sunday afternoon," he counseled me. "It's not good to live your life alone."

After my two years here in France, I had an enviable apartment, interesting friends, even the offer of a professorship in Paris teaching women's studies. The various strands of my life were finally weaving together. Why leave now? That old recurrent battle percolated once again inside me: love and security versus freedom and adventure.

The cabby's words touched a sensitive spot. Since the feminist movement, many of us had given up the old ways of being women, but we hadn't quite figured out the new guidelines: It was like floating through space without a ripcord to pull. Sometimes it was lonely out there. Occasionally I felt like coming in for a landing.

At the airport, in the crush of the crowded waiting room, I nudged my possessions toward the check-in counter: two oversized suitcases, three cartons, and a portable computer. I felt like a contemporary version of Hannibal crossing the Alps—minus the elephants.

"*Madame, s'il vous plaît,* may I help you?" A dignified man in a tweed jacket appeared beside me. For a moment I expected a Maurice Chevalier refrain to spring from his mustachioed lips. His kindly face was lined but robust, sophisticated, and attractively sensual; his pepper-and-salt hair, well-cut wool clothing, and perfectly shined mahogany cordovans announced substance and dependability. Like a hero from a fairy tale, he exuded an otherworldly serenity.

We chatted our way up to the counter. "*Je m'appelle* Alain de Kervoisin. Shall I see if I can arrange our seats together?" Somewhere over the mid-Atlantic, it became clear this could be the start of something. He was a baron from northern Brittany, tracing his ancestry back to the Romans. He had two chateaux left, was land-rich and cash-poor, and raised what cash he needed by selling off lumber from his forests and raising trout. I felt as if we were acting out a Henry James novel: I the young—well, not that young—naïve but energetic New Worlder; he the highly cultivated, somewhat jaded and fading European.

The narrow seats encouraged our shoulders to touch. When he poured my wine and toasted to our serendipitous meeting, the sides of our hands brushed ever so slightly. I had never known a man like Alain; in his early sixties, he was sixteen years older than I.

By the time the flight reached our destination, I had offered to delay my departure for San Francisco for a few days to help him explore New York for the first time. He had the use of a friend's vacant apartment on the Upper West Side of Manhattan, and I stayed with old friends.

"One of the reasons I've come to the States is to establish connections with antique dealers," he said. At the Metropolitan Museum of Art, Alain taught me about the nuances of the furniture collections, which helped me to look at small curves and carvings with a new awareness. I tried to concentrate on the collections, but more absorbing were how the lines of his jaw and cheeks changed from shadow into light when he spoke. How amusingly his elegant dignity contrasted with his brightening demeanor when I touched his hand or said, "What fun you are to be with," or "I've never known a man like you."

Just around the corner from the furniture collections was one of my favorite rooms in the museum. "Come look at the Temple of Dendur. This was a goddess temple. Did you know that in pre-Christian times, to make love with a temple priestess was considered a sacrament?" He opened his eyes wide at this bit of information.

"Well, well. Now it's time for some tea, don't you think?"

Our week together passed swiftly: towering corned beef on rye at the Carnegie Deli; a Broadway musical, *42nd Street*; elegant and romantic small restaurants; a boat trip from the Hudson to the East River; more museums; and finally, slow and precise lovemaking in his temporary apartment. I had never made love with a man so much older than me, nor one of Alain's background. He too seemed a bit nervous the first night I went home with him.

"Let's have a drink. I quite like your American bourbon." He quickly downed one glassful and poured another. He embraced me gently, kissing me in a preliminary way as though he were testing the waters, then more firmly, opening my lips with his tongue. His immaculate manners extended into his lovemaking. Slipping off his clothes quickly, he slid under the sheets. As I undressed, he pointedly looked away, then welcomed me to join him under the covers. In my travels, I have found that lovemaking techniques vary according to culture, class, and age of participants. This was my first time with a French aristocrat, and I was not disappointed.

The following month, when I was back in San Francisco, along with the first signs of spring, letters and cards began to arrive on both sides of the Atlantic. Our writing, like our conversations, moved back and forth between French and English, which was perhaps emblematic of our striving to bridge emotional and cultural ravines.

"*Belle Dame,* I don't forget you," he had written shortly after our January meeting. "I keep a very pleasant memory of our romantic encounter and I would like to renew it. Love and kisses, Alain de Kervoisin."

Finally in May, I found myself writing: "*Cher Alain, Merci* for your wonderful letter and the sprig of lavender. It still has a beautiful scent and makes me think of spring in the French countryside. . . . In just thirty days, I will be back in Paris and look forward to accepting your invitation to visit you in Bretagne. I shall let you know when I have a clearer view of dates and so on. . . . *Je t'embrasse.*"

And so, after a few months of exchanging letters, the summer found me in Brittany at the Manoir de Kervoisin. Alain met me in Paris and we drove out to his manor. Tall rows of plane trees formed bowers over our heads as we entered the long driveway. On the right stood a small, abandoned but perfect half-timbered chateau dating from the fifteenth century; Queen Anne once stayed there. Opposite it stood the fairy-tale cottage in which he lived; this had been converted from an ancient water mill. Behind the cottage were laid out more than seventy enormous tanks in which trout were bred and raised. All around the cottage and into the distance were well-tended landscaped shrubs, flowers, and vegetable gardens. The sound of running water from the tanks permeated the air, as did some slight odor of fishiness when I stood amid the pools.

"During the winter of the great floods twenty years ago, all the trout escaped," Alain recalled. I looked at the open-air tanks teeming with swarming trout, the dense population arranged according to size and age. Never again would I bite into a fresh pan-fried trout served with small white parsleyed potatoes without remembering those trout swimming in the shit of a thousand other trout.

I thought about the fish suddenly liberated from their suffocating confinement during those floods. What a surprise for a trout to be suddenly swimming in flood tides, with much of western Brittany as its sea. Did they long for the safety and surety of their tank? Or did they relish chance encounters and freedom—until the floods receded and they found themselves stranded, out of their element?

"Monsieur le Baron!" My short course in pisciculture was interrupted by a medieval-looking farm hand wearing a large yellow rubber apron, baggy overalls, and brown rubber boots that came up just above his knees. The worker's ruddy, carbuncled face reflected many years in the rains and winds of Brittany. With his pale blue eyes, muscular forearms, and thumb in a dirty bandage, he could have just slipped out of a Brueghel painting.

Alain gave instructions to his servant concerning the feeding of the fish, removal of equipment, and preparation for tree cutting. Alain's limberness and vitality belied his sixty-four years. He told me his ancestors dated back to Roman times via Flanders, and his two chateaux had been in his family since the fifteenth century—but that titles and land did not necessarily translate into cash. Unfortunately, since they were more than five hours' drive from

Paris, the chateaux and trout farm were almost unmarketable. So, with his modest stands of oaks, his trout-breeding operation, and his vegetable garden, Alain lived a life out of time and almost totally self-sufficient.

The warm sun soothed my travel-weary shoulders, and drowsiness seeped through me. I felt more content within myself than I had in a long time, safe and cared for.

"*Venez. Venez. S'il vous plaît.* Come in, please, I want to show you my mill house, my cottage." Alain used the ancient Breton word *penti* for cottage and always addressed me with the formal "*vous.*" It was part of his traditional old French ways. When I mentioned it, he explained it reflected the respect and esteem he felt for me. At first, such formality seemed odd, but, as I became accustomed to it, I too felt myself playing into an appropriate role: no longer a visitor from California, but a special woman, selected by chance to be here, playing a part in this tale.

The water-mill cottage was painted pale salmon, with gray stone corners and dark timber trim; it was covered with vines and pink and red climbing roses. Crossing the curved bridge to the front door, the air, scented with the sweetness of roses and herbs, caressed my cheeks. The inside of the cottage had the feel of a place that had been lived in and well tended for centuries. In the large stone fireplace a fire crackled, illuminating Alain's guitar, easel, writing desk, and book-lined shelves.

The typical French country kitchen contained an old stove, a gray stone sink, and fresh green vegetables gathered in a basket. A row of windows overlooked a small orchard of fruit trees and flowers. I felt as if I had come home to Grandmother's house—but instead of Grandma, here was this lovely man who might have just walked off the screen of a Hollywood version of a French romance.

Later Alain removed an antiquated grilling rack from the wall beside the living room fireplace and used it to cook our steaks over the fire. He sang and played old tunes for me on his guitar, including "*Il y a longtemps que je t'aime. Jamais je t'oublierai.*" This song always touched me with its poignant mix of sadness and hopefulness concerning the possibility of love. Over our cognacs, he said, "Have you ever thought you might marry again?"

I paused. Probably that Parisian cab driver was right. Love, continuing and unconditional: This is what mattered in life. On the other hand, marriage had long seemed to me a trap, and I usually spoke against it. Somehow here, in this peaceful atmosphere, with this kind and interesting man, it didn't seem such an impossibility. What would it be like to be a *baronne*? I could actually follow my dream and move to France—but in a very different way than I had envisioned.

"Maybe. I don't know. I haven't thought about it," I said.

Certainly Alain seemed healthy and stable, as well as generous and considerate. Even lovemaking had a flair; it was almost like being at a fancy dress ball or tea party—but feeling at home there. It was passion without lust, intimacy without sentimentality, total pleasure without concern for past or future. It was like the best of conversations with the closest, most interesting of your friends. One morning as we embraced in his large bed, pushing aside the bolsters, I complained that the long, narrow, cylindrical cushions gave me a stiff neck. He joked: "French pillows haven't changed since the eighteenth century. But I'll find you another pillow. Let me show you something though; these bolsters work quite well in certain positions." Proceeding to demonstrate, he pushed one under my hips.

Someone once joked that little French boys are taught to be good lovers right along with their history and grammar lessons. Our orgasms came and went with pleasure but without disruption of a larger flow of communication. Alain explored my body with care, tenderness, and genuine interest—like visiting a new country. His body was taut and fit; the maturity of it excited me. How much of life it had experienced, like the collected memories inside his chateau. Making love with Alain was like being in that ancient space. Confinement with a great view. I called him *mon petit chou*, my little cabbage, a term of endearment usually used by parents for little children. It seemed so totally inappropriate for a man of his dignity that I found it amusing. After all his years alone since his wife had left him, twenty years before, something inside Alain was touched and pleased by this intimacy. "Oh," he would cry out in surprise when I spoke to him in this way. "*Non, c'est amusant.* Continue. I like it."

There was one odd thing about Alain's body. Through the fleshy part of his left upper arm was a hole. The wound itself was long healed, but a small indentation tunneled through the tender flesh. Alain explained that during the war he had been a freedom fighter. One day out in the Breton woods, a Nazi bullet had come his way.

That was all he would say. He quickly changed the subject whenever I mentioned it and pulled away when I touched his arm.

Mid-mornings, we walked together through the enormous gardens, collecting vegetables for the soup that Alain made for lunch. The pink, towered castle that dated from the fifteenth century fascinated me. It was really a miniature chateau, but was still a building of considerable size. Alain used it only for storage, as it needed much restoration within to be habitable. "I would love to see the inside of the tower," I remarked.

The heavy wooden stairs, which curved up to the second story, were indented from centuries of footsteps. Since most of the windows were barely more than slits through the deep walls, fortress-like, it was dark, and we had to grope our way along. At the top, an enormous room contained piles of boxes and, surprisingly, a rowboat. "Ah, yes, these are my books from earlier times. I no longer read these sorts of books. Now I have much work to do, much to study."

"What do you mean?"

"My work, with the gypsies; I'll tell you about it some other time. Oh, my, yes, *amusant, un bateau dans une tour, n'est-ce pas?*" (How funny, a boat in a tower.) Alain changed the subject. The large, unfinished room was like a room in a dream, its ancient rafters dusty, strung with cobwebs. Hundreds of boxed books surrounded the very landlocked boat. One end of the room gave onto the circular tower. The ancient planks sank slightly as we moved about. From the windows of the tower, I could see almost 360 degrees around, over the trout ponds, forests, pink water-mill cottage, the flower and vegetable gardens.

"Why don't you come live here? You could work up in this tower. I would restore it for you. You could even have a horse. The riding is excellent through the woods around here." As always, I loved imagining my way into other lives. What peace there was here. And the possibility of real love, companionship, an idyllic life. It would certainly be a leap of faith to give up the life I knew, my work and home, and make a permanent move to a new country at this point in my life. Would I feel like Rapunzel if I accepted?

"*On va voir.* I'll need to think about it," I said as I hugged him.

A few days after our visit to the tower room, during lunch outside in the garden, I asked, "What is this about the gypsies?" He poured some more wine into each of our glasses.

"Part of every year I spend down near Avignon *avec les gitanes,* with the gypsies. I help to teach the gypsy children. I play my guitar. I live with them for a few weeks at a time. And I bring them to . . . a better way."

"What do you mean?"

"Him." He pointed overhead to the Breton sky. Over the last years, he explained, he had fully embraced Catholicism. "Oh, yes, it's very helpful, very helpful." When we went inside, he showed me a current pamphlet from the Catholic Church. "It guides me away from offensive or troubling books, movies, and television programs—those that are disturbing to my beliefs."

Gradually, I was becoming aware that Alain was perhaps only being patient with me, waiting for the best moment to push me toward religion. Those outside of Christianity or Judaism were, he felt, lost. One afternoon as we walked past an old synagogue in a small French village, he asked me if I wanted to enter, referring to my Jewish heritage. "You should try," he said. "After all, you are among the chosen people."

Some months later back in the States, while I was sitting in a Berkeley café, describing Alain and the hole in his arm, a Jewish friend remarked, "You know, Nazi sympathizers were sometimes identified with such marks." He didn't say how he knew this. Was there a connection between Alain's Catholic work and some hidden guilt concerning his activities during the war?

When I criticized Le Pen, the infamous radical right-wing politician, to Alain, he said he agreed with Le Pen's *"La France pour les Français"* (France for the French) and had voted for him in the last election. "Did you know," I teased, "that Le Pen's ex-wife has revealed in the press that he bleaches his hair blond to look more Aryan?"

"Arrête. No politics, no religion. Remember?"

The summer was coming to an end. On one of the last days before I left for the States, we drove to the coast and visited old fishing villages. The late summer sun shone its false promise. After a lunch of wine-soaked mussels, we felt very relaxed and almost groggy as we strolled around the port. These ancient harbors were like museums for the rotting old carcasses of well-used fishing boats. The gray weathered wood revealed the ribs and core of the vessels. Looking inside them felt almost illicit. Once I had had a dream in which I was invited to look inside myself and could hear, see, and feel the sounds and sights of my own internal organs at work.

Looking into these old boats reminded me of that dream. Somehow the whole experience was beginning to feel like a waking dream.

"I want to show you the marshlands while the tide is out," Alain said. From where we left the car, we had to walk a long way to reach even an inch or two of sea. The seaweed formed slippery, brown, changing patterns as the tide began to come in. At the bottom of some cliffs, there was enough depth to swim. Alain had carried our swimsuits and towels in a small bag. The water was very cold. "I bathe here most of the year," Alain said as he plunged in. After a very brief dip, I climbed to the top of the cliff.

There they were, just as I had seen them in archaeological photos. In large concentric circles stood the menhirs, ancient and mysterious stones from before the time of the druids. Some of them were etched with vulvas and breasts. What kind of a civilization had lived here? Until recently, no one had paid much attention to the female aspects of this early culture. My own work had moved toward the study of women in ancient cultures. So far I had not been able to get Alain to be curious about or even accept the validity of such a pursuit. "If I were a geologist studying stones, you would respect that," I said to him.

"That is totally different. That is science. This, what you talk about, is . . . ah, come on. Remember, no politics, no religion," he reiterated.

Maybe he was right; perhaps I was proselytizing him, even as I objected to his efforts to draw me toward Judeo-Christian religious beliefs. Gradually, I hoped, he would respect and show interest in what I did. I touched the stones gently and lay on my back among them, staring up at the clouds, which were starting to blow in rather rapidly.

"Hurry. The tide's coming back," Alain called. I clambered back down to the flats. Alain took my hand and, as the water started up our ankles, we began to run. I had never seen a tide come in so rapidly. The sound of the gurgling, rushing water was hypnotic. I looked ahead to where our car was parked, up at the top of a steep cliff. It was at least a mile away. Alain was certainly in better shape than I— he ran easily, and I was already winded. It was thrilling to be swept along at the edge of a natural pattern in this way.

Soon another pattern swept me back to California: teaching commitments, my other life. Always there was that questioning edge. Like the sea brink where the waves approach and recede, whispering backward off the beach. I pictured life out of time: writing in Alain's tower, walks among the tide pools of Brittany. Would I begin growing my hair long, planning an escape from that charming captivity? And Alain, a reincarnation of a medieval prince, drawn to a modern woman. While Alain drew me out of my world into the peace and rhythm of tides and harvest, I drew him into the pleasures of the body, which he had long denied himself. Perhaps he was beginning to question some of his rigid views. For each of us, these challenges, while intriguing, might prove more than we could bear. Yet the promise of love, home, a coming to rest, a real rest, arms to entwine and comfort: These longings were of course within each of us.

Seven years passed. Work, travel, family deaths occupied me. Alain and I spoke from time to time, wrote perhaps once a year. My mother's death marked the end of my now totally dwindled family. His words: "Don't forget me too soon. *Je vous adresse trois pensées* without limit: *Promesse Tendresse Caresses.*" Later: "Charming and Sexy Lady: I love the seascape of San Francisco that you sent me. I send you a compass to help you negotiate in the fogs which must be quite bad there. . . . Let me hear from you. I hope to have news soon of your return to France. . . . Your P.C." (*petit chou*). I understood that his gift of a compass was a reference to his notion that his views were more clear-sighted than mine.

One day something made me pick up the phone and dial Alain's number. A woman answered, apparently a servant. "I will ask *Monsieur le Baron* if he can come to the phone."

"It's you? No, no. I am sick. Don't call me anymore."

Stunned, I hung up the phone. Was he really ill? I sensed some anger in him, a disappointment with me.

Later that summer, I visited friends in their farmhouse in Lussan, in the south of France. With the self-assurance and intuitiveness of a French woman in affairs of the heart, my friend, when she heard about the latest installment in the Alain story, said simply: "You must write him immediately. Don't refer to the phone call."

Within two days, a response to my letter was in my friend's mailbox. "My Fairy Lady. Come to me as soon as you can."

Two trains later, I stepped out onto the *quai* at St. Amboise des Bois. I felt excited and a bit nervous. As though in a slow-motion film, Alain and I ran toward each other from opposite ends of the train platform. His face had a few new lines, but he appeared to be healthy and trim. "You look wonderful, even younger and more beautiful," he said, still the charming Frenchman. "Hurry. We must get home. The haying must be done today and I have no help, can't afford to hire anyone. Anyway no one works properly. I must do everything myself."

Later, at lunch, Alain looked at me: "When I saw you last, you seemed more confused. You had some deep unhappiness inside your soul. Now you seem more calm." He continued: "There is a part of you I detest, a part of you I like, a part of you I love. This still continues to be the case."

He was in a pensive mood, and apparently had been so often in recent years. He began to play his guitar for me and to sing. I loved the sound of the music and the French language, but his religious songs made me uncomfortable. "What about some Jacques Prévert?" I asked. He switched easily to French love songs.

"You warm my body and my soul, my love." That particular song, its deep tones and eternal longing, always made me shiver.

He placed his guitar to one side and looked off into the distance. "It was so odd, you know, I had my small heart attack in the place where we swam together, near those old stones. Fortunately some people were walking along the beach and pulled me out.

"I want to tell you the real story about the hole in my arm. During the war, I was very much in love with a woman who lived in Paris. I was sent off to the German front. I realized I should have proposed marriage to her before I left because I knew there was another man; he was there in Paris. Of course, I couldn't just leave my squadron. So I shot myself in my upper arm. I had intended it to be just a graze, but I misjudged my aim. The result was a serious wound. But it did give me a medical leave, which had been my intent all along."

"So did you go to her?"

"Yes. But as I had feared, she had already accepted the other man's offer of marriage. It was one of the great sadnesses of my life. *Je n'ai pas eu de la chance dans ma vie.* So much has not gone right in my life." He recounted a litany of situations gone awry throughout the years.

A few days later, we had a dinner at the coast of the rose granite. *Le granit rose*: a place I had loved years before. The sun set behind the small island just off the coast, outlining a small chateau with gold and rosy hues. As we walked along the coast, Alain said, "Those stupid pagan stones. Let's go in to dinner." In the restaurant, he complained about the slowness of the service. "I have my three-minute rule. If they do not come to us in three minutes, I get up and leave."

The next morning was Sunday, and I suggested we visit some of the Breton Pardon festivals that were occurring. Religious in origin, these festivals were now a mixture of good times, ancient dances, and traditional foods, such as crunchy Breton waffles. At the town of Guingamp, women strolled in long black embroidered dresses wearing elegant starched lace caps on their heads. Dignified men in black suits, some with beards or mustaches, stood about. Soon the main parade would make its way through the town.

Alain parked on a side street, across a large square from the main gathering place. As he turned off the ignition, an urge welled up in me: a sexual urge, as well as, perhaps, a desire to test my own power. There was something exciting to me about the mingling of ancient earth religions counterpointed by the repression of them by modern Christianity. Both these forces were so strong within Alain. Unwilling to contain myself, I touched his thigh, then between his legs, and pulled him around me. "My, my," he said in not unwelcome surprise. Tightening my upper thighs around his, I pressed myself against him. We both rocked and moaned our way to satisfaction. Intermingling with our cries were the ancient strains of Breton music—flutes and drums and bagpipes. Grinning, I looked at him. He pulled himself back together. "Ah, what tedious music. Let's hope no one has seen us. Come, we shall miss the parade. You know this is a very sacred religious gathering." It seemed appropriate that we had made love in the car next to a festival that combined the very elements that were the stuff of the attraction and conflict between Alain and me.

Back on his estate that evening, I watched two doves on the roof outside edge closer together. The breeze that came in tasted of autumn. *L'heure bleue.* Dusk was all around me. In the morning, fog covered northern Brittany. *"La brume est arrivée hier soir,"* Alain said. All was fog and mist as I looked out—it was like gazing down upon a great cloud. No more green land, no sea.

I needed to think about what to do.

I decided to return home.

❦

From San Francisco, I wrote Alain, suggesting that, before it was too late, why not come together as best we could, share those parts of our lives that we could, give each other love and comfort? The years were passing. I recalled someone once telling the story of a tired Amazon who decides to take off her armor and rest, but discovers that it has become attached to her skin. I didn't want this to happen to me.

About ten days later, through my mail slot tumbled a very large and full envelope. Opening it, I found a postcard photo of *la côte de granit rose*. Taped to the back of the card was the Christian Credo. *"Voici ce que je crois*. This is what I believe. It is for me the most important thing in the world. It is totally and absolutely incompatible with your own beliefs. No more plans between us appear to be possible. *Oublie-moi*. Forget me. A." I poured the envelope's contents onto the table. Ten years of my letters and writing lay before me.

Perhaps I always knew that I was pushing him too far, pressing the passions of ancient memories into his own beliefs. It was precisely this conflict that had been enacted on this land as the ancient stones and temples of the earth goddess were toppled by the new religions.

How would Rapunzel have felt if, when she finally let down her hair, the prince tried to cut it off? A kind of reincarnation of a medieval prince with antiquated ideals, not fitting into any world, Alain was left alone, which is perhaps where he always wanted to be. And I had free-fallen into a sea where love and freedom were on opposite shores. We had both drifted out on a tide that had no ebb.

Digging Dordogne

Ericka Lutz

"I believe that this great peaceful region of France will always be a sacred spot for man and that when the cities have killed off the poets this will be the refuge and the cradle of the poets to come. It was most important for me to have seen the Dordogne: it gives me hope for the future of the race, for the future of the earth itself."

—*Henry Miller,* The Colossus of Maroussi, *1941*

In 1980, I spent six weeks in the Dordogne, working on an Upper Paleolithic archaeological dig in exchange for food and a place to pitch my tent. France's southwest was a long way from Northern California for a nineteen-year-old. The Direction des Antiquités Préhistoriques sent a treasure map: a single page of instructions with a train schedule. From Paris-Austerlitz to Limoges, from Limoges to Périgueux, from Périgueux toward Agen to Le Buisson. Take the bus toward Sarlat, get off at Saint-Vincent-de-Cosse, and walk back two hundred meters to the unpaved driveway on the right. The letter told me to bring a sleeping bag, an air mattress, and a tent.

At nineteen, I was disconnected and impatient, stuck in the desperate layer between childhood and adulthood. Almost two years before, I'd moved from California to New York for college, but college didn't "take." I joined and left a Trotskyist sect, quit theater (my lifelong passion), dropped out of school and moved into an East Village apartment, had a bad love affair, then fled back home—all within nine months. For the next year, I sat in my attic room in my parents' Marin County cottage house and wrote poetry. The universe stretched before me with too many possibilities. My cat died. I waitressed. I played pool in gay leather bars. I took a French class and fell in love with a simple and beautiful young man as aimless and lost as I was. Too much—and nothing—happened.

And then my uncle, an archaeologist, offered respite from my vague desperation, hooking me up with a French colleague who took on student volunteers each summer at his dig. It could have been anywhere, France or Zaire or Kansas, and it would have been enough. But France! The sophisticated land of Henry Miller, Babar the Little Elephant, Edith Piaf, fondue, and wine had gleamed on the horizon beyond my reach. On the basis of that single sheet of Xeroxed instructions, I bought a plane ticket and threw myself back into the world.

On my way to the dig, I spent three days in London, culture-shocked, jet-lagged, and thrilled to be in Europe. But by the time I got to Paris, I was cowed. Despite my French class, I did not know the language. *"Je voudrais un jus d'orange,"* I carefully said to the waiter on the train from Calais to Paris. "Oh. Do you mean you want an orange juice?" he smirked. My train out of Paris didn't leave for three hours, but I didn't know how to stow my backpack and I didn't know the right words to find out. So for three hours I sat in the station—Paris, in all its glory, right outside the large arched doorway.

The train trip south was uneventful and beautiful. We crossed mountains and forests and fields. Small towns rose and fell. At dusk, I sat waiting for the bus in a small medieval village beneath a stone church, listening to the bells clang and eating bread and cheese. Yes, I thought. Now I am someplace. I got off the bus and found the driveway easily. Up the dirt drive, I joined twenty other people at La Beynaque à Bézenac, the old farm that housed the excavators for this particular dig every summer. Jean-Henri, the site director, lived in the farmhouse; we pitched our tents in a nearby field, showered in a camp shower, and ate in the barn. Above the farm, a small fortress-like chateau hung ghostly in the moonlight.

Jean-Henri worked us hard. The bell clanged every morning at 7:40. I lay on my back in the old army-navy pup tent and wiggled into jeans or cutoffs. The breakfast bell rang at 8:00—we drank bowls of coffee and ate tartines of bread four inches wide and twelve inches long, studded with farm butter and smeared with jam from earthen crocks passed up and down the rough-hewn farmhouse table, which seated thirty. At 8:30, the first vanload of excavators left. Twenty minutes later, the van returned for the rest of us, taking us up into the forested hills on winding narrow roads paved with crushed yellow-white limestone. We hiked on foot the short distance to the excavation site, an *abri*—cave shelter—hidden under a limestone overhang.

All summer, I sat in a one-by-one-meter square, deep in the pit, and scraped and brushed at dirt undisturbed since the Aurignacian period, twenty-five to thirty thousand years ago. The dirt went in the bucket. Anything I found—stone, bone, flint—I measured and logged in my notebook. I drew the artifact—blue with red crosshatches for burnt bone, black for flint—and then wrapped and labeled it and passed it over to Jean-Henri or one of his assistants. When the bucket was full, I climbed out of the site to a high overlook where I sifted the dirt through a large sieve. I labeled and logged anything I found in the sieve.

As I sifted dirt, I gazed out over the chateau-topped hills. A single electrical wire looped down the valley near a two-lane road where an occasional slow car passed, driven by a farmer in a beret. Subtract the electrical wire and the road, and it could have been three hundred years ago. There, in the clearing below this stone fortress, that fairyland castle, knights once jousted. In the shallow bend of the river, occasional remnants of the Hundred Years War surfaced in the form of old coins and bent armor. Subtract the chateaux (the British on this side of the river, the French on that), and the hills rolled as they had three thousand years ago—Bronze Age artifacts hid in shallow graves. Ten thousand years ago, twenty thousand, thirty . . . during the Ice Age, the glaciers came to the edge of this valley and stopped, thawed by the beauty and peace.

This view had always been the same.

I climbed back down into my hole and continued to scrape my way back in time. It was strong medicine to sit in a hole and scrape slowly at the same patch of earth; enforced patience was the best cure for chronic impatience.

The other dig participants were French, American, English, Canadian, and Belgian students and graduate students: Joe from South Carolina, Dan from Tulsa, Doug from Iowa, Kathy from Santa Cruz, the girls from Toronto, Laurie from North Harrow. We sang as we worked or talked quietly or dug silently, accompanied by the sounds of scraping and birdsong. At noon, the van brought us down the hill back to La Beynaque through a village of limestone and walled streets so narrow that the van's mirrors scraped against the walls. Marie-Claire, the camp chef, laid out bowls of rice and tomato salad, soup, goat cheese from her goats, bread, coarse country pâté, duck confit or mutton stew, potatoes. We poured local red table wine from brown pitchers decanted from five-gallon jugs. The unfiltered wine left thick sediment in the bottom of our cups and stained our teeth, tongues, and lips purple.

At 1:30, the van took us up the hill again, where we worked until 6:00; dinner was a lighter meal—with more wine. On warm evenings, we sat on a grassy slope and watched the stars or the phosphorescence of the glowworms. On rainy nights, we huddled in our pup tents and read by flashlight, wrote letters home, and slept. The days found their rhythm.

My first weekend there, Von, the American assistant director of the dig, chose me for his "summer girl." Von had a fiancée in New York, but they had, he told me, an understanding. He was the sexiest man I'd ever met. He was dark and tall, with one side of his face a little different from the other where he'd wiped out on a motorcycle on the back roads of the Dordogne two years before. I'd watched him all week—the archaeology bad boy, the dig stud, brilliant and going places. We drank wine late Friday night and outlasted the Canadian girls until even Georgia got the hint and left us watching the glowworms and he kissed me. We had sex in his tent. Too drunk, I fell asleep halfway through—he roused me and I wandered across the field to collapse in my own sleeping bag.

The next day, Von took me hitchhiking past the ruined fortress of Richard Coeur de Lion (now owned by a broke nobleman who was slowly renovating the castle) to the medieval city of Sarlat. Von chatted in the regional patois with old men in their

Deux Chevaux who picked us up. I sat quietly while he talked about his plans for his dissertation. The *chat* seemed to have gotten my tongue; for all my boldness in seducing him the night before, I was shy, inexperienced in holding conversations with an older man.

From Sarlat, we hitched through the hills to Rocamadour, a medieval village known for its walnut liqueur and tiny *cabouchons* of nutty goat cheese. Above the village, a stone stairway led up the hill to a chateau and continued past the ramparts up to a cathedral. Every year, pilgrims seeking healing mounted these hundreds of stone steps on their knees to pray to the Black Virgin. On the way home, it rained, and I felt hungry, tired, and impatient to be back at the farm. Few cars passed, and it took a long time to catch rides. Again, I was quiet in the car. Every time I thought of something to say, it sounded stupid, so I didn't say anything at all.

By the time we got back to La Beynaque, it was clear that Von and I were no longer together, though he never told me why. He quickly chose a new summer girl—a new arrival to the dig, Brenda, a cute little bird from England. I thought she looked chubby in her string bikini. But at least she could talk to him, and at least (presumably) she could stay awake. He didn't speak to me again for the rest of the summer.

I felt baffled and enraged, chosen and discarded. I was not used to being ignored. France *was* romance—how dare he throw me back in the sea as if I were a too-small lobster? For a couple of weeks, I tried to trick Von into acknowledging my presence. I stalked him at

the dinner table; he moved away, never meeting my eyes. I gave
Brenda the evil eye. I posed for Doug from Iowa in cutoffs and a
halter top near where Von could see us. I cried on the shoulders of
Sylvia, Georgia, and Patty, three Canadians who'd never had
boyfriends and did not understand. Von, gorgeous and unattainable
to me, sat at the other end of the farmhouse table—the good end—
and laughed with the good people. I sulked loudly, the summer
drama queen, brokenhearted. Here I was, too frightened to take
advantage of three hours in Paris, too inept to have a love affair in
France. The sophistication and wild experience I sought from this
country, these people, fell through my hands as I grabbed for it.

As respite from my angst, I immersed myself in the excavation.
My work was good, my site journal perfect and neat. I enjoyed the
details of the work, the discovery of secret worlds extrapolated
from fragments and shards. I made my entries carefully, imagining
Von reviewing my notes during the winter in New York; an image
of my laughing face and naked body would come into his mind,
and he would bury his face in his hands in regret. I still desired
him. I replayed his compliments. He'd found me cute, liked my
smile, my zest. He was wrong to dismiss me so abruptly. I wrote
him letters in my tent at night. I didn't give them to him.

From the farmhouse, in the dark, came light and music and
laughter: Jean-Henri was hosting a party for Wendy (his "summer
girl") and Von and Brenda. Out in the field, I got drunk with Dan
from Tulsa and Doug from Iowa, on a heinous mix of grain alcohol,
lemonade, and wine. I woke violently ill, the tent rocking, the world

spinning. I moaned for my mother. Tents opened and shut around me. In the morning, purple vomit dotted the hillside.

We worked hard, but evenings, nights, and weekends were our own. One night we looked for the small ghostly castle that hung above the farm, driving on narrow roads etched in the forest-covered cliffs through dark valleys of walnut and oak. We didn't find it. One weekend we hunted mushrooms—chanterelles and *cèpes*—in the woods after the rains. Marie-Claire let us into the farmhouse kitchen to scramble eggs with our fungi. She taught us how to make French eggs, stirred lightly, not whipped, with a little water and salt. We sautéed the mushrooms in butter and added them in at the end. The hard breads we ate that summer, flat and big around as my arm, stood stacked to the ceiling in the low, whitewashed kitchen.

Marie-Claire let us into the kitchen only one other time. The Canadian girls and I spent Saturday harvesting cherries from the loaded trees, and Marie-Claire made jam from the glowing fruit. I tasted a cherry while the jam was cooking. Then another. She shooed us from the building, but I couldn't stop. I snuck again and again into the kitchen, scooping ladlefuls of the bubbling fruit and burning my tongue, sating myself, feeding myself the sweet fruit. The syrup dripped from my mouth; her jam turned out watery. I overheard the scene in the kitchen, Marie-Claire shouting in French. At dinner, I knew from her narrowed angry stare that she suspected me, but I gazed at her with innocent eyes and she turned away. We spread watery jam on our bread for the rest of the summer. They kept the kitchen locked after that.

Other weekends, Jean-Henri took us on field trips. The painted caves at Font-de-Gaume, the carvings at Cap Blanc. Beneath the dark limestone, we cast our flashlights at the walls to see the animals dance. Traveling through the countryside one afternoon, we arrived at Domme at dusk. In *The Colossus of Maroussi*, Henry Miller wrote, "Just to glimpse the black, mysterious river at Domme from the beautiful bluff at the edge of town is something to be grateful for all one's life." I tried to experience Domme fully, but I was too angry and sad—Von and Brenda strolled hand in hand on the cliff. I didn't try to speak to him anymore. I huddled with the Canadians, hating that, in this paradise of beauty, I cared about something so petty. France lay before me through a pane of glass; I could see its promise of high culture and self-confidence, but I could not touch it.

As the summer wore on, my mood flipped between ecstatic and lonely. The other members of the team, though older, seemed more naïve than me. They were from rural areas, they focused on their studies. I'd dropped out of college, spent my time cocktail waitressing in smelly bars while they got good grades, drank beer, and tipped cows in cornfields on the weekends, or whatever good college students did. What would I do when I left this place? My future lay ahead of me—empty and bright and dark. In my journal, I folded a piece of paper with addresses of places to work in Germany (the Black Forest), in Paris (Shakespeare and Company bookstore), in Switzerland (ask René at the Youth Hostel Grindelwald and try St. Moritz, Zermatt, and Lepsin for tourist season work), in Israel (the youth hostel in Tel Aviv will know about jobs on a kibbutz).

Somehow, though, the layers of beauty and time surrounding me—in the coarse feel of the earth, the old bones I picked up and catalogued, the sky, the hills and cliffs, the fields and forests, the slow dark river—managed to penetrate. The Dordogne River wound through the verdant valley of grapes and walnuts and farms, the black-stained limestone cliffs. Lying in my tent on Sunday mornings, I listened to the bells ringing down the valley from medieval village to medieval village, closer and closer and closer and then ours—St. Cyprien, and then Beynac and Sarlat and farther away . . . then the thunder and rain came down the valley, too, like gunshots and bomber jets.

After dinner one night, six of us drove to a cave with wall carvings just discovered behind a pigeon coop, where they had been hidden for centuries. "Unpublished," the others said, enjoying the thrill of that word. We drove a long way on roads without streetlights. The moon was dark, and we got lost in the hills. It was almost midnight before we arrived at a small farmhouse. The entrance to the cave was a small hole high in the pigeon coop—strong men hoisted me up until I could crawl through on my belly into a narrow *grotte*. We trained our flashlights on the walls, tracing the carving of a giant mammoth, partially eradicated, right above us. The hills hide thousands of cave sites, and this one would never be a tourist attraction. Archaeologically, it wasn't significant, but the night and the cave's silent intimacy thrilled me. How many people had seen this? How many ever would?

Von and Roger played their strong lights around the cave, high and low. And then, right next to me, shoulder high, Von's light picked out a small mammoth, six inches long, carved hastily in the soft limestone. A single line delineated the mouth. The mammoth smiled. Sixteen thousand years ago, an artist had stopped to entertain a child.

We stared in silence. Anyone who sees the painted caves of the Dordogne and surrounding areas—the leaping bison; the reindeer licking a smaller deer's head—knows that these were gentle masters at work. The animals arc in joy; the shading is extraordinary. Yet it was the care and humanity in the baby mammoth in La Grotte de la Mammouth, beyond any other magnificent art that we'd seen, that moved me to tears.

Scrape the earth, scrape, scrape, all day in my hole, deeper and deeper in time. The drama of my failed romance faded away, and my brain, circling my life like a vulture, slowed and relaxed. Scrape. I felt the chink of a piece of flint. Brushing and scraping the dirt away until the top lay exposed, I uncovered a small, pale-green arc three inches long. I logged its position, drew its shape. I picked it up from where it had lain in the ground for twenty-seven thousand years and held it in my right hand, rounded side cradled in my fingers. The bottom was still crusted with dirt. My thumb swept across to clear it and fell into an indentation, thumb-shaped. I was holding a flint knife, crooked comfortably in my hand, ready for use. Time blurred—the last person to hold this, twenty-seven thousand years ago, had held it in just this way. This sensation, this weight, the smooth coolness of the stone, had felt the same way in that person's hand, and I experienced a direct link. There was no past, no present, no time in between, just me and that other person, sitting here, in the same place, holding the same tool.

That sensation, that smooth, cool link across time, would remain long after the summer was over and I'd gone on to other adventures, where I gained the worldliness and confidence I so craved. It stayed as a reminder of the layers of reality all around us, below the angst of the moment. It helped me forgive myself for being so foolish. It resonated in me, along with a deep love for the valley that had cradled me for six weeks in its peace and beauty and timelessness.

"France may one day exist no more, but the Dordogne will live on just as dreams live on and nourish the souls of men."

—*Henry Miller*, The Colossus of Maroussi

A Prenuptial Visit
to Chartres

Dalia Sofer

I sat with my sister on the edge of the arcade on rue de Rivoli, facing the barren trees of the Tuileries garden. It was dark still, and wet. A shimmering frost covered the empty streets and sidewalks—the previous days' snow was beginning to freeze, and jagged icicles hung like teardrops from the corners of the shops' misty windows. Behind us, an old man was sweeping the walkway under the arcade, the swish-swish of his broom the only sound at that early morning hour. This was our last day in Paris, and we had just missed the 7:00 A.M. tour bus that would have taken us to the Loire Valley.

We'd been coming to Paris together since we were children, a few times with our parents, later on alone. At first we came because experiencing the city concretized what we'd been learning all year long in our French school in New York: Molière and Hugo, Proust and

Breton. We would watch plays at the Comédie-Française and stand in awe in front of Proust's house—now a bank—on boulevard Haussmann. In the summertime, we'd head to Gibert Jeune in the *Quartier Latin* to stock up on smooth-papered Clairefontaine note-books and ink cartridges for our fountain pens. Later, when we were no longer in school, or even in college, the two of us still made the pilgrimage to the bookstores and stationery shops dot-ting the Left Bank, justifying our juvenile purchases as rare gems not to be found in New York. Now, with my sister's impending wedding looming over us, I knew that this would be the last trip we'd take together, like this.

We got up and made our way down the ghostly street. At the place des Pyramides the golden statue of a heroic Jeanne d'Arc on her horse glistened in the morning dew. The wind was brisk, biting my face every now and then. I was surprised at how cranky I felt. I usually wasn't the type to get worked up over a missed tour bus. But the sight of the dark, desolate square in front of the tour agency that morning, and the agent accusingly shaking her head, repeating her phrase—*Vous êtes en retard!* (You are late!)—with a righteousness not unlike that of my high school principal, had left me feeling hollow.

We settled at a round table by the window in a café and ordered coffee and croissants. The place was warm and bright, and my shoul-ders loosened under my heavy coat. A few early risers slumped over their cups of coffee and morning papers at the bar, while the bar-tender wiped plates and cups with his towel, stacking them one on top of the other for the morning rush of caffeine seekers.

"How about Chartres?" my sister said.

I dunked my croissant in my coffee and watched its papery leaves crumble into the warm liquid. Somehow we'd never been to Chartres, despite its proximity. I remembered, from our high school history classes all those years ago, the bizarre affinity my sister had had for flying buttresses and all things medieval.

"Sure," I said. "Let's go."

Chartres was a one-hour train ride from Gare Montparnasse. By the time we stepped off the train, the morning had completely unfurled and the sky had somewhat cleared. Few people were on the streets. Chartres is a sleepy town, and except for the cathedral, there is little reason to go. On a cold and windy day, even the cathedral cannot expect many guests.

We walked at a leisurely pace toward it. I was now glad that we'd missed the tour bus. I realized the last thing I wanted was to be dragged along with scores of shutter-snapping tourists from one Loire chateau to another, to be told to look up, then down, then to the right of an armoire, then to the left of a bedpost. Here, the day stretched before us in the town's stillness.

On the way, my sister had told me how good our trip had been for her, how it had given her a break from all the wedding planning. It was true that during the previous months, wedding-band demo tapes and sample invitation cards had overrun her life. Bridal magazines encroached from every corner of her apartment—the apartment the two of us had shared until her engagement—from under the bathroom sink and from over the radiator and from behind the blender. I too had been dragged into the whole affair, buying stacks of invitations emblazoned with Victorian teacups for the requisite women-only shower and discussing painstaking transportation plans with overanxious guests.

"Tomorrow it'll be back to reality," she said.

I tried not to let that reality further dampen my spirits. Strangely, it was only here that I'd gotten all gloomy about her wedding. Back home the wedding was just that—a wedding.

As we got closer, I could make out the cathedral, a massive edifice of stone and glass, with its mismatched towers and green copper roof, overlooking the town. Many centuries have left their architectural mark on this monument, beginning with the twelfth and ending as late as the nineteenth. We walked around it once, savoring the marvelous medley of rounded Romanesque arches and severe Gothic vaults. A chorus of flying buttresses, jutting out of the cathedral's side like sturdy ribs, rooted it firmly in the ground.

Inside, we stood small before a maze of intersecting vaults and stained glass. Only the echo of an occasional footstep or the accidental clink of a visitor's necklace hitting the candelabra interrupted the silence. The smell was characteristic of most cathedrals—a mixture of wet stone and incense and time. I had read somewhere that the Gothic cathedral, with its ribbed vaults and long transepts, was inspired by forest glades. Nowhere did this seem more true.

We said little. We walked around, taking in as much as we could in our brief visit. The sun must have come out, as rays of light were now dancing in the nave, reflected through the prism of the stained glass windows above. A strange calm filled me as I watched my sister, standing some twenty feet away and looking up intently at a glass painting, nursing some private thought. I wanted to return to the first time we came to Paris together, in our early teens, when every aspect of the city—the arching bridges over the Seine, the labyrinth of narrow streets in the Marais, or a young man carrying a bottle of wine in the six o'clock light of the afternoon—all seemed to carry furtive messages, suggesting endless possibilities for exploits, exciting us with that pure joy peculiar to adolescence.

We returned so many times because there was something wonderful about being young in Paris—disappearing inside shops and emerging with items we could afford thanks only to overextended credit lines, spending hours in bookstores and returning with stacks of books that we knew we should have read long ago and that we probably never would, spending entire afternoons at sidewalk cafés and talking amid the incessant puffs of our fellow idlers. At night, showered and perfumed, we strolled to our favorite restaurants, relishing the knowledge that we were lovely to the men who passed us by. We knew, of course, that in many ways Paris is a city like any other, with its own urban problems of pollution and congestion and immigration. But to us, none of that mattered. It was just a place where we could escape for a while, together.

I walked to the nave and stood under the converging lights. This nave, I told myself, was the end of our exploits. It was our terminus.

We left the cathedral filled with the tranquility one feels after a restful sleep. We found a café, ordered some tea. "Maybe I should have become a medieval scholar," my sister said. We laughed, both of us knowing that the days when a lifelong commitment to Chaucer or Villon seemed like a viable career option were long gone. We leaned back in our chairs, lazy in the glare of the afternoon sun. She pointed at the teapot on the table. "Isn't it gorgeous?" she said. It was lovely—an oval silver pot ridged with serpentine curves, its sides reflecting the distorted images of the other diners and the yellows and reds of the room. I smiled, knowing that in her mind she was already decorating her marital home with this very teapot.

Paris Can Wait

Lori Oliva

The forest of Compiègne was damp with the mist that had covered France's far northern countryside since I'd arrived, four days earlier. As I trudged through the mud, water seeped into my shoes, chilling my toes to the bone.

"Why didn't we stay in Paris?" I asked my friend Charles. He seemed a bit annoyed by the question, so I quickly reminded him that he was an obnoxious American, too. It wasn't so long ago that he himself had wrangled his belongings into a backpack to head off into a journey of self-discovery.

Back in Paris, I thought as I trudged, I would have embraced the bitter weather. We would have sat inside a dimly lit café taking hummingbird sips of espresso, elbow to elbow at tables shaped like mushroom caps. We would have nodded at the comings and goings of Parisians, and I might have noticed the weave of the rattan chairs as I listened to Charles, my best friend, who has lived in Paris for more than five years. He would have told me how he wakes each morning to the scratching sounds of street sweepers or how dark French chocolate rivals the density of its Belgian counterpart. He would have told me how he loves the sarcasm of the French as he corrected the waiter who referred to me as Madame. *"Mademoiselle,"* Charles would say. We'd have laughed as the waiter raised his eyebrow and apologized with a grin that told me that, while my days of being a young miss are long gone, I will always be a youthful maiden in my mind.

We would have browsed the merchant stalls selling books on the banks of the Seine and reminisced about how we'd made crepes for our high school French class.

Back in Paris, the dreary weather would have been the perfect backdrop for watching Sorbonne students, artisans, businesspeople, loners, and tourists bustle down alleys and brave the cutting, wet cold, armed only with umbrellas and raincoats.

But instead, this November 11, we were trekking through damp, muddy woods less than sixty miles north of the French capital. Charles wanted to make a pilgrimage this armistice holiday to Bruges, Belgium, and en route, to these mucky woods, which he called the "Birthplace of Veterans Day."

As far as I knew, Veterans Day referred to a national holiday declared in 1954 by President Dwight D. Eisenhower when he changed the name from Armistice Day to Veterans Day. But to me, this day had no location. It was a time to pause and reflect on the men and women who had served our country in wars, and perhaps take in a parade or watch Shriners drive their go-carts down Main Street, USA.

I had never given much thought to the origin of the date. However, Charles, who had lived among the French, for whom the two world wars had much more immediacy, knew the details. Armistice Day, as it is still called in France, is celebrated on the anniversary of the treaty that was signed in 1918, at the eleventh hour on the eleventh day of the eleventh month in the forest of Compiègne. The French would never attempt to change that date, as the Americans did in 1968, when Congress changed the holiday to the fourth Monday in October. But even in the United States, the historical significance of that date, November 11, aroused enough protest to force Congress in 1978 to restore the observance to the original date.

Our wet hike was taking us to a clearing in the woods, where, as Charles's demeanor promised, that historic import would be driven home. However, my fear of catching a deathly cold was momentarily taking precedence over history. I took comfort in the fact that we weren't the only ones hiking through the woods to the site, which is actually in Rethondes, just outside of Compiègne. As we made our way toward the glade, we were among throngs of people, who greeted each other with courteous nods as they sidestepped frothy puddles and overhanging branches.

I lifted the last of the rain-soaked tree limbs and unleashed another cascade of droplets upon my head. Standing before me was the Clairière de l'Armistice, the "armistice clearing." Surrounded by tall cypress trees, manicured shrubs, and towering stone statues, the glade was an inviting oasis in the thickly wooded bog. Its open space called for exploration. As I walked toward the array of memorials, my stomach did a nervous dance, as if a series of unpleasant memories were about to be unleashed.

"It is here that World War I ended," Charles said.

Perhaps weaned on too many Hollywood versions of war, I had always imagined the end of the Great War proclaimed at Versailles. I had envisioned the world leaders gathered around a gold-leaf table, sitting in red velvet chairs, holding large plume pens in their hands as they signed the treaty. The real picture was more complex, if less grandiose. In this clearing, France's Marshal Ferdinand Foch had embodied the hopes of France, Great Britain, and the United States by dictating to Germany peace terms—some rather harsh—that called an end to World War I.

A recap of the toll on life underscores how desperate those hopes must have been, on all sides of the conflict. The United States, a latecomer to the war, lost more than 116,000 soldiers in just over a year of combat. Still, it was a fraction of what the French lost—more than 1.3 million lives—and the Germans, who tallied 1.7 million dead.

Charles and I followed the white gravel path that led to the heroic statue of Foch. Standing two stories high, Foch cut an imposing stone figure as he overlooked the clearing. A general surveying his troops, he gave the impression that at any time he might step off his stone pedestal and resume his command.

As Charles explained, it was Foch who dictated the strict 1918 peace agreement to Germany in his makeshift office, a railroad car that was originally housed below his statue. Today, in its place on an abandoned railroad track, sits a raised stone slab inscribed with words reflecting deep-rooted sentiment:

"HERE ON THE ELEVENTH OF NOVEMBER 1918 SUCCUMBED THE CRIMINAL PRIDE OF THE GERMAN EMPIRE—VANQUISHED BY THE FREE PEOPLES WHICH IT TRIED TO ENSLAVE."

Not far away, a sculpture of the German imperial eagle lies face up, twisted and fallen, its wings spread ignominiously in defeat. A gigantic sword pierces the bird's body, its lifeless head falling off the stone pillar. It was a disturbing sight even for one who was not aware of its full meaning and bitter irony.

Despite the many years that have passed, these powerful symbols catapulted me back to November 11, 1918. I looked upon the clearing, manicured and stark, and thought about the men and women who'd once walked these grounds. Suddenly the dampness was less annoying, and the cold gusts that knifed my skin reminded me that soldiers had braved the same elements to serve their countries.

"So this is a tribute to the end of World War I," I said to Charles, truly moved.

"Among other things," he said vaguely. He cocked his head and pointed across the clearing to a tiny railcar that stood alone, a football field's distance away.

"Is that the railcar?" I asked in excitement. I grabbed Charles's hand and led him through the crowd to take our place in line. I imagined Foch and his French delegates sitting in the same leather-bound chairs that would soon be within arm's reach. Only in Europe could such an artifact be so accessible.

"Not exactly," Charles answered. "The original railcar was destroyed by the Germans. This is a replica."

"Oh," I said, confused. I watched the rain bead against the railcar's newly painted steel. *How could Germany destroy the railcar when they were the ones who'd surrendered and lost the war?* Trying to hide my ignorance, I leaned toward Charles and whispered, "I don't understand. Isn't this a place of peace?"

"Not entirely." I knew Charles well enough to understand when he wanted me to learn things for myself. So we proceeded up the steps and entered the coach. The crowd was pressed together so tightly that we were forced to keep moving, shuffling through the cabin while trying to take in as much as possible. My eyes scanned the 1918 armistice, which dictated the hardball terms to Germany—occupation of its country, a ban on its air force, and the seizure of its coal mines. The pens used to sign the treaty were displayed under glass, along with uniforms, flags, newspaper articles, and photos that catalogued the construction of the monuments and a tiny museum that housed Foch's original railcar.

It was at the second set of photos that I understood the meaning of Charles's last remark. A chill ran down my spine colder than the day's wintry gusts. Documents representing a new victor and dated June 22, 1940, more than twenty years after the end of World War I, were displayed throughout the tiny museum. A photo of a large swastika-emblazoned flag draped over the statue of the impaled German eagle was disturbing, as were others—of a bulldozed wall of the museum that had housed Foch's railcar, and of the tiny office-coach taken from its shrine and placed back on the tracks where it had stood in 1918.

In 1940, German troops blitzkrieged their way into France, and, in an act of revenge, Adolf Hitler, his pettiness and destructiveness at full tilt, chose the forest of Compiègne as the site for the French surrender. It was here that Hitler humiliated the French by having them sign over their country—in the exact same location that had once given them their freedom. Members of the French delegation found themselves aghast in the railcar—face to face with Hitler, sitting where Foch had sat to dictate the terms of the 1918 armistice.

The last photo in the 1940 series showed the attempt by the Germans to erase the site of the armistice, which had brought only a brief respite between two wars. The entire glade was destroyed; pathways and roads were plowed up, trees cut, and the original museum demolished. The photo captures the barren wasteland, with the exception of Foch's statue, which was left untouched—one can only wonder why—and standing witness to the destruction of the monuments that had once stood for victory and freedom to the French people.

As I took in the sequence of events, I was enraged anew by Hitler. These photos represented not only the first documented account of Hitler's reign in France, but proof of his intent to enslave every country he conquered.

After the invasion of Normandy in 1944, Compiègne was liberated and returned to the French. Near the end of the railcar, a final series of photos and small brass plaques details the reconstruction. German prisoners of war were put to work to rebuild the roads and grounds they had demolished. By 1950, the glade was restored to its original condition and a coach that replicated the original armistice railcar was donated by Wagon-Lits Co. The words inscribed on the last plaque are those of the 1956 French government: "In the Armistice Glade, the desecration is now effaced."

As I made my way toward the exit, I peered out the last of the brass-framed windows. I watched as curious tourists, veterans dressed proudly in uniform, families, and schoolchildren eager to experience history trickled in from the wooded paths.

It was in that moment that the surrealism brought a sense of overwhelming clarity.

These people were not only paying tribute to those who had served their countries, they were visiting a destination that would lead them to reflect on the act of war itself—the violence, the oppression, the loss, and the determination to overcome. Every day Europeans are forced to remember the destruction brought by two world wars—by bullet holes in their cathedrals, bronzed monuments of soldiers struck down in battle, and concrete buildings that dot their medieval villages as a part of the postwar reconstruction effort that rebuilt thousands of thirteenth-century structures lost in countless bombings.

However, what I felt that day was the sheer will of one country to remember the tyrannical acts stemming from one man's evil and the undying determination to surpass it.

"Thank you for bringing me here," I said to Charles as I buttoned up my parka and stepped back into the drizzling rain.

Madame Michel

Susan M. Tiberghien

It was summertime when we arrived in the small village of Istres, with its white walls and red, sun-baked roofs, built on a hillside in southern France not far from Arles. My husband, Pierre, was assigned to the Air Force base hidden in the vast fields of lavender surrounding the village.

I was an American bride learning to be a French housewife. We had met as students in France three years earlier. Then Pierre followed me to the States. We married and returned to his country.

In the fifties in Provence, there were no supermarkets, no Colgate toothpaste, no Coca-Cola, no paper bags. Each day I bought a baguette at the bakery, cheese at the dairy shop, meat at the butcher's, vegetables and fruit at the open-air market. And each day I carried it all home in my straw basket.

There were no refrigerators, either. I kept the milk in an earthenware pitcher, wrapped with a damp dish towel, outside on the windowsill. The mistral, the strong dry northerly wind, cooled it even on the hottest of summer days. There weren't any washing machines. I washed everything in the bathtub, including the sheets and towels. They dried in no time on the line outside the window, near the milk pitcher.

During my apprenticeship, I learned to count on my next-door neighbor, Madame Michel, an imposing woman twice my age and twice my size, steel-gray hair in tight ringlets, corpulent and corseted.

Shortly after my arrival, I rang her doorbell. As an American accustomed to greeting neighbors, I wanted to introduce myself. Slowly she took me under her wing.

"*Pauvre petite dame,*" she said, "here all alone, with a husband away day and night at the air base."

My French made her scowl. She tried for over a year to teach me to roll my r's. I already found it difficult to make them guttural; now my next-door neighbor wanted me to make them *provençal* at the same time. I tried but knew I'd never succeed.

When Madame Michel learned that I was expecting my first baby, she told me about *her* first baby—how huge he was, and how she thought she was going to die right on the kitchen table in her house. She said that after that, she made sure there'd never be another. She shook her head and turned her attention back to me.

"You should eat garlic," she said, "raw garlic, every day." She told me it would keep my muscles supple and ease the delivery. I nodded and hoped my muscles would stay supple without the garlic.

She suggested we go garlic picking every Friday morning. It grew wild in large clumps near the fields of lavender. We pulled it up by the armful. On the way home, she'd tear a bunch apart and squeeze out the cloves for me to chew on. At first I tried to say that I would wait for lunch, but soon I just stuck the cloves in my mouth and chewed along. The taste was sweeter than the scent.

Madame Michel found my husband very handsome in his Air Force uniform, with the gold-buttoned jacket and gold-trimmed hat, and invited us to Sunday dinner, requesting that Monsieur come "fully dressed." Laughing, Pierre explained that that meant in his full dress uniform. Madame Michel wasn't a churchgoer, but said she'd hold dinner for us until after Sunday Mass.

When we rang at her door, she was dressed in black as usual, but for the occasion she was wearing a polished yellow stone that glowed fiercely on her bosom. In the dining room there lingered a musty odor mixed with lavender. Three places were set on the starched white cloth.

"I've made a surprise for you," she called from the kitchen. "*Paella provençale.*"

She carried in a large round earthenware dish. Yellow saffron rice was ringed with onions, tomatoes, olives, and mushrooms, and in the middle rested a rabbit's head, its eyes staring straight at me.

"That's the best part of the *paella*," said Madame Michel. "There's one eye for each of you."

Pierre and I declined. I quickly looked away, but not soon enough. She had picked up the rabbit's head and was sucking out each round, beady eye.

It was a very cold winter. Our landlord told us it was exceptional. But Madame Michel went to call on him, insisting that he install something to heat the apartment and keep us from freezing.

"Imagine, the baby coming and no heat!" she said. In her house she had radiators, but she never used them. She said it wasn't worth the fuss since she lived alone.

So our landlord came and put a wood stove in our kitchen. When Pierre was home, he tended it. When he was working at the air base, Madame Michel tended it. Certain that her American neighbor knew nothing about French wood stoves, she'd watch for when I was alone, and then come tapping at our door.

Soon she was poking around in the potbellied stove, shoving the wood back and forth, and sure enough, the fire would glow for the rest of the day.

One Sunday morning, I woke up to a snowstorm. Pierre was away at the air base, and Madame Michel was hammering at the kitchen door.

"I thought you'd freeze and never wake up," she said, carrying in an armful of wood.

When I told her I was late for church, she said it didn't matter. People didn't go to church when it snowed. "Besides," she chided, "you're getting too pregnant to go to church, snow or no snow. In your condition, you shouldn't show yourself so much."

I told her I was still going to go. She shook her head disapprovingly and said something I didn't understand and wasn't meant to. I bundled up warmly and trudged up the narrow street to the old stone church built when the village was more prosperous and its people more churchgoing. With the light snow falling, everything was still and pristine.

The church was nearly empty, and I huddled up front with a few other people. The priest arrived late, his black cassock and black beret flecked with light flakes of snow. He told us we had gained in the grace of the Lord and could now go back home. There would be no Mass.

Shortly after the snowstorm, I started having labor pains, and Pierre drove me to the hospital. The birth was long and laborious in spite of Madame Michel's garlic. Pierre fell fast asleep while reading Marcel Pagnol aloud, but I was no longer listening.

When finally the nurse wheeled me into the delivery room, the doctor was long gone. Only the midwife, short and squat, was still there. As the pains shot through me, I thought of Madame Michel on her kitchen table.

The midwife told me to push harder. She pushed with me until at last it was over, and the baby was born. It was a boy. We named him Pierre, after his father and his grandfather, and chose William as his middle name, after my father.

Madame Michel came to visit. She appeared awed, almost afraid. She said it was the first time she had ever set foot inside a hospital. Staring at the baby swaddled in white in the small crib, she quickly brushed away tears.

"Maybe I should have had another baby," she said. "But not on the kitchen table."

I never learned where her one son lived. He had moved away long ago, that was all Madame Michel told me. And she never told me anything about her husband. Whenever the subject came up, she'd fall silent.

She lived alone in her house with dust covers on the furniture, though she must once have had several people at her large table. The sounds and smells were still there in the shadows, along with the china, crystal, and silver. Ancestors were looking down from the dark walls. The chandelier hung low. Candlesticks were waiting to be lit.

"I don't have much company anymore," she told me.

Whenever I asked her to come and have supper with us, she always refused, saying she was better off keeping to herself.

And every night I watched her light go out in the kitchen at nine o'clock sharp.

In the springtime, my husband watched her hoe and plant a vegetable garden on her side of the fence. Madame Michel told him he could come and help her. She said he could turn over the earth in the corner and plant whatever he wanted. He asked if she knew any-thing about planting corn.

"Corn," she repeated, looking at him as if he'd lost his mind. "What are you thinking of doing with corn?"

"I'm thinking of eating it." He explained that he had tasted it fresh from his father-in-law's garden in the States. "It was sweet and tasted a little like fresh green peas."

"Well," she said, shaking her heavy shoulders in disbelief, "you just try eating the corn that grows around here. It sure isn't sweet peas."

We wrote to ask my father how he planted his corn. An enve-lope of pink grains arrived along with a sheet of handwritten instructions. Pierre made ready a patch of earth and planted half of the package.

Madame Michel stood watch as ten cornstalks raised their heads out of the ground. Soon one cob of corn appeared on each stalk. Madame Michel would pull back the husks, just a little at a time, when she thought I wasn't looking, and take a good long sniff of the kernels.

Once the corn was ripe, she finally accepted an invitation to Sunday dinner at noon. I picked six of the cobs and served them steaming hot. Madame Michel didn't say much. She was too busy chewing every kernel off her cob, and off the extra three ears.

Before we were to leave the village, Madame Michel wanted to make us another *provençal* dish.

"No rabbit this time," she promised. "Only fish. I'll make you a real bouillabaisse, *bouillabaisse provençale*. Invite some of your friends and I'll come make it for you."

This way, she added, I wouldn't need to move the baby and carry him next door. She told me that babies should stay put, especially in the evenings. She scolded me plenty, but she hugged me, too.

"Then you'll stay and eat with us," I said.

"No, not in the evening."

The day of the bouillabaisse, she arrived early in the morning with bundles of fish, bought at the market and wrapped in newspaper. She undid them at the sink and started splashing away, slitting open bellies, slashing off heads and tails. Blood, scales, and other bits splattered around the sink and over the wall. I disappeared into the bedroom to nurse the baby, closing the door behind me.

Madame Michel was still at the sink when I came back. She held up each cleaned fish by its head and rattled off the names: "*raie, rouget, rascasse . . .*" I wondered if she had purposely chosen fish whose names began with "r." She set them aside to be cooked at the last minute, put everything else into my biggest pot, and told me to let it simmer all day.

When she went home at noon, I washed down the wall and opened the windows wide.

She came back in late afternoon to make the *rouille*, a garlic and red pepper sauce, grinding it into a fine paste with a pestle in an old wooden bowl she had brought with her. I opened the window still wider, the aroma of fish now infused with that of garlic. From time to time she'd taste a bit on her finger. Then she'd taste a spoonful of soup. And then she'd dip in one of the croutons she was making and taste that, and then another.

When finally the seasoning was right, the soup strained, the fish cooked, and the croutons golden, I asked her once again to stay. She shook her head and said she'd eaten enough. That evening, our friends tasted one fish, and then another. They dipped the croutons into the *rouille* and savored the soup. And we toasted Madame Michel.

It was soon time to pack our belongings and leave Provence. Pierre had finished his military service. We were moving to Brussels, where Pierre was going to work for the Common Market. I was going to find supermarkets once again—Colgate toothpaste, Coca-Cola, and paper bags—and central heating and people speaking English.

I never liked leaving a place. I always wanted to take it with me. And so I wanted to take along Madame Michel, the wood stove, the corn patch, the *paella*—without the rabbit's head.

We found the little package of pink corn grains that my father had sent us from the States and tried to give what was left to Madame Michel.

"Oh no," she said. "I wouldn't know what to do with it."

Our small car, a gray 2CV, was packed. We didn't have any furniture; just ourselves and our first baby, along with the straw basket for shopping and a few odds and ends for keeping house that I had found in the village.

Madame Michel came to say goodbye. She looked at us and sighed heavily. "Now be off with you."

She hugged little Pierre, or Peter, as I was calling him. She let big Pierre kiss her on each cheek. And then she clasped me close in her strong arms.

"*Adieu, ma petite dame,*" she said. "I'll miss you. I never had a real neighbor before."

Paris Revisited

Constance Hale

Monsieur de Méneval was not the type I'd expect to see on all fours: a small, graying Frenchman, crisp of carriage, with an astonishing aquiline nose. And this was not a place that promised such informality—a bourgeois *salon* with its large oil portrait of an austere ancestor, its ancient bandoliers marking the walls with X's, and its glass cabinet filled with such empire relics as pieces of royal china and a fan from Empress Eugénie.

"*Le voilà,*" he called out ebulliently, lifting a lithograph from the bottom of an ornate chest so that my mother and I could see. There, on horseback, was Napoleon III, reviewing his troops. And there, just behind him, was M. de Méneval's "*arrière-arrière grandpère*" (great-great-grandfather), Napoleon's private secretary and the guy who'd earned the impressive "de" in the family name.

I had never imagined, when I impulsively invited my mother to Paris for her sixty-fifth birthday, that we would end up here, in Versailles, sipping tea and chatting in French with Claude and Monique de Méneval. Sure, I had long known that my mother's junior year abroad had been one of the formative experiences of her life. But hadn't she moved on, settling for a humble life in rural Hawaii, never returning to France, letting her ties loosen?

She had, in my view, not so much abandoned her taste for all things French as passed it on to me. She'd pulled me off the beach to read *Madeline and the Bad Hat* and *Eloise in Paris*. She had bought me a small spiral notebook, inscribing its brown cover with MON PETIT CAHIER DE FRANÇAIS and listing words for me to memorize. Although our everyday diet consisted of things like tuna-noodle casserole and Hamburger Helper, she occasionally gave my brother and sister and me a taste of her Continental past by serving a cheese soufflé or chocolate mousse. Once or twice she treated us to stories of the French gypsy who'd taught her to read palms—and then proceeded to predict our futures.

Tales of gypsies were eventually supplanted by tales of the Baron Louis de Méneval, scion of the *petite noblesse,* and the *baronne,* head of their formidable household in the seventeenth arrondissement. Long on pride and short on funds, the enchanting de Ménevals had chosen the socially acceptable way to improve the family cash flow—by taking in a college student. My mother must have fit the bill perfectly: She had studied French all her life (even winning a statewide award in Ohio), but she wasn't just a French nerd. Raised by a socialite from Massachusetts, and named "Madeleine" after her, she had followed in her mother's footsteps and attended Smith College. But by then my mother had lost *her* mother, and she always spoke of the de Ménevals with a fondness usually reserved for family.

Now here I was in Versailles, connecting the dots: Before me were all the possessions that had filled my mother's descriptions of her "home" in France, inherited and put on display by the eldest son of Baron Louis and the *baronne*. And here were the intersections between a family and a country, whose history Claude was proudly enumerating. Here, too, was the relationship between Claude and my mother: The once stiff rapport between a competitive twenty-three-year-old law student and a smug twenty-one-year-old American girl was now reinventing itself as a warm friendship between a retired businessman turned Napoleon expert and a photo-toting granny from Hawaii. But, more than anything, here were my mother's deep ties to Paris that, because they preceded me, had remained largely a mystery.

The longing for such connections had sparked the idea of our trip. Then, midway through the planning stages, my father was given less than a year to live. Though he and my mother had been divorced for thirty years, the news devastated us both. We considered postponing, until a new urgency swept aside our misgivings. *Go. Now. While there's time.* In the face of losing Dad, I yearned to draw closer to Mom. Planning the trip got me through some hard months.

And there was lots of planning. With the help of the Internet and two Paris services, we finally selected two pieds-à-terre: a large studio on the Ile de la Cité and a one-bedroom on rue du Fer-à-Moulin, in the fifth arrondissement. Apartments would afford us corners of privacy and our own washing machines, and their kitchens would give us an excuse to load up on fresh bread from Poilâne, cheeses from Androuët, and mustards from Hédiard.

But having apartments also let us experience Paris not as tourists but as residents. Staying on Ile de la Cité meant waking to the eight o'clock bells of Notre Dame, lunching in the lovely place Dauphine, taking in an evening violin concert at Ste. Chapelle, and snagging ringside seats for the Saturday-night street theater, kicked off by nine guys in surgical scrubs and a gay man in a bunny costume with a few strategically placed fresh carrots, green foliage flopping. In the fifth arrondissement, we visited with the *boulangère* down the block, blazed through the rue Mouffetard market every day, and took mint tea in the Arab Café de la Mosquée, with its blue-and-white-tiled fountain, fig trees, and round brass tables.

Mom spent one morning on the Ile de la Cité scouring the map. Soon she was leading me across the Seine on a footbridge, around the tiny chapel of St. Julien-le-Pauvre, and then straight to rue de la Huchette, a narrow medieval alley. She stopped in front of a crude stone façade.

"My dear friend David brought me to the Caveau de la Huchette on my birthday in 1953," Mom mused, casting a glance at the Greek restaurants now lining the street. "This was just an old alley then, with centuries of grime." Pointing to pictures of dancers on a subterranean parquet, under stone arches, she continued: "Steep, turning steps descended to a cavelike room. Sidney Bechet and his Blue Notes were playing! A gang of men all dressed in black turtlenecks—they were called 'apachés' then—arrived. One of them—very handsome— asked me to dance. At first I demurred, but David insisted I dance with him. By chance I was wearing a black cashmere turtleneck and a flared red skirt. He was very polite with me. And he was the most wonderful dancer—the smoothest . . ." I sensed in Mom's voice the hint of something dark, forbidden, thrilling; later I learned about the underworld of the apachés and the rough tango they practiced.

"Afterward, in the foggy mist from the river, David and I circled around a small Greco-Roman church. We walked back across the city to the seventeenth, past bakers in basements—one blew flour at us from a bellows. We crossed the place de la Concorde, completely empty. I was carried part of the way because my feet hurt."

And so I started to learn the secrets of my mother's time in Paris, to become familiar with the subterranean corners of her history. And she, in turn, learned mine.

My Paris is a place of unfamiliar longings suddenly made all too familiar. A place of romance witnessed from a distance (those kids kissing on the bridge), and loves unrequited. A place you can desire but never possess.

Mom knew little about my having fallen in love in my early twenties with a French photographer. Jacky and I shared poetry, love letters, and, briefly, a room in a sprawling house on the St. Cloud train tracks. We had met in San Francisco, but it was in Paris, after a ten-month separation, that Jacky took me up in his bearlike arms, burrowed through my jumble of curls, searched for *"le creux de ton cou"* (the hollow of your neck), inhaled deeply, and whispered, *"Je retrouve l'odeur de Connie"* (I am rediscovering the scent of Connie).

It was also here that Jacky and I made our own Odyssean journey on foot, starting at 1:00 A.M. from Châtelet and ending at 4:00 A.M. near the Bois de Boulogne, when Jacky gently let me know that he intended to live alone, that he needed to *be* alone. An artist needs *la solitude*, he said, without a trace of grandiosity.

And now, fifteen years later, Jacky was inviting us to an exhibition at the Canadian Cultural Centre of still photographs he had taken for a film, *The Red Violin*. There, he added, we could meet Nam, the French-Vietnamese woman for whom he had abandoned *la solitude*, and their son, Ulys. Never was I so happy to have my mother's company. I was struck by uncharacteristic shyness; she held my hand while I gazed at photos, she made small talk with Nam, and she praised Jacky on the handsomeness of his son.

Jacky's first words to my mother—*Je la connaissais quand elle était toute petite* (I knew her when she was a little girl)—called Bob Dylan to mind (not just the line "she breaks just like a little girl," but also

"I was hungry, and it was your world"). And they also reminded me of that peculiarly French brand of intimacy—witty, affectionate, and brutally detached. He looked better than ever, his auburn hair brushing his shoulders, and I found that I was still susceptible, still able to be pulled in by his tender words and then spat out into the dark Paris night.

My mother did not directly address the whirl of confusing emotions within me as we left the cultural center and wandered past Les Invalides. "Would you like to stop by that wine bar you've been curious about?" she asked instead, with exquisite delicacy, placing her hand softly on my shoulder. And so we submitted together to the attentions of Au Sauvignon's proprietor, who determined that we should leave his establishment having tasted the very best France has to offer.

As Mom and I continued to explore the mysteries of Paris together, we continued to refine our mother-daughter act. It started with the language we both love. Mom's French is formal, correct. Mine is informal, current. With the artists and boutique owners in Village St. Paul, I chatted away as Mom intently listened. I could see the wheels turning in their heads, could see the scenarios spinning. *The mother must be French—trim figure, strong nose, elegant sweep of white hair. The daughter's French is good, yes, but the unkempt curls, the running shoes, the earnest manner! Not French, no.* Then I mashed a few pronouns, Mom answered a question, and their stories shattered around us like dropped Limoges.

Not that I did all the talking. In an antiques store in the Marais, an eccentric, leather-skinned patron pointed me downstairs to his collection of '40s French soap wrappers. (Flat, light, and cheap, *etiquettes de savon* are the perfect souvenir.) Having dispensed with me, he extravagantly set two director's chairs in the doorway, facing out, and flirtatiously invited *"madame"* to join him *"sur la plage"* (on the beach).

To track down the de Ménevals, Mom had pored through an old phone directory, thinking that at least the children—Claude, Françoise, Christian, and Bébé—would still be in Paris. She found a Claude de Méneval listed. I dialed the number, identified myself, and asked after Claude. The man who answered—he was much too young to be a contemporary of my mother's—explained that Claude, once a roommate, had moved to Poland. "Perhaps you are looking for the father," he added. "I believe he lives in Versailles."

And so we ended up at the train station near the famous palace. The moment Claude stepped out of his blue Renault, my mother gasped. "He hasn't changed at all," she whispered. He and my mother approached each other without a trace of doubt, clasping hands and kissing on both cheeks. Then we got into the car; I joined two towheaded and very curious little boys in the back seat. Unlike Claude, who retained the formalities of the seventeenth arrondissement, Monique was a down-to-earth Bretonne at ease welcoming us into their modern townhouse on the edge of Napoleon's woods, passing delicate porcelain teacups and crisp cookies laced with chocolate, and firmly insisting that the grandchildren, Luc and Daniel, sit still.

After an exchange of gifts and the finding of the magnificent lithograph, Claude suggested a tour. Mom had visited the palace years ago, so for this tour she chose the gardens. All six of us piled into the Renault while our private guide, who had spent his retirement learning about this place, revealed the intrigue behind the endless canals, the Grand Trianon, and Marie-Antoinette's faux peasant village. When we parted, the Paris my mother and I now shared had acquired one more facet.

On our last night in France, Mom and I treated ourselves to *Turandot* at the Opéra de la Bastille. We arrived early and bantered with two young, idle ushers. Hearing that Mom had come back to Paris after forty-five years, they asked excitedly, "What was Paris like in 1954?" and "How do you find it different?" She answered in French, basking in our interest, telling us how *belle* it is now, the trees ever more majestic, the façades scrubbed of coal dust, the shadows of World War II banished, and the men in green keeping the boulevard St. Germain spotless.

In Act III, we both wept quietly in our front-row balcony seats as the slave-girl Liù expressed her "deep, secret, unconfessed love" and anticipated her untimely death. We wept for the loss of Liù, for the pending loss of my father, for the loss of youthful romance, for the loss of rekindled friendship, for our last moments together in Paris.

To console ourselves, we stopped at the Café le St. Médard for a crème brûlée, a last look at the crowd, a last listen to the fountain. There I realized I had lost an earring. It was half of a pair of lovely mabe pearls, traced in gold, given to me by my father on my recent birthday, the last I would spend with him. I was momentarily heart-sick, and then realized that an earring was the only thing I'd really lost on this trip, and that I could live with that.

A few weeks later, back home in California, a small gift arrived from my mother. It was a pair of pearls.

Paris Noir

Monique Y. Wells

Jean-Pierre Jeunet's 2002 romantic comedy *Amélie* sent tourists in droves to Paris's artists' quarter, Montmartre. I wonder how many of them knew that, in addition to being Amélie's neighborhood, it was also the home territory of one of America's foremost writers, Langston Hughes.

Hughes was one of many Harlem Renaissance writers who sought his muse in Paris; Claude McKay, Countee Cullen, Gwendolyn Bennett, and Jessie Fauset were others. Their paths seldom overlapped, but they all were influenced by their experiences in the City of Light.

Their visits coincided with the heyday of the post-World War I jazz scene that developed in a triangular patch of the city immediately below the boulevard de Clichy and in the shadow of the butte known as Montmartre. This area came to be known as "Black Montmartre." The area where Hughes lived, which was on the butte itself, encompasses the idyllic rue Lepic, the place du Tertre next to la Basilique du Sacré-Cœur, and the rue des Trois Frères.

As an African American and a ten-year resident of Paris, I thought it fitting to celebrate the 100th anniversary of Langston Hughes's birth, February 1, 2002, by reading about his life in Paris and retracing his steps here. Armed with Hughes's autobiography, *The Big Sea*, and Arnold Rampersad's biography, entitled *The Life of Langston Hughes, Volume I: I, Too, Sing America*, I set out to walk the route that Hughes took to Montmartre on his first day in Paris.

I began at the church of Notre-Dame-de-Lorette in the ninth arrondissement, which Hughes passed as he headed up the hill to the area in which the first African-American community in Paris was established, after World War I. Notre-Dame-de-Lorette was built during the nineteenth century, when the bourgeoisie from neighboring Faubourg Poissonière moved westward to a new quarter called Saint-Georges. Though the church was constructed to provide the growing population of the new neighborhood with a place to worship, its name was quickly transferred to the many women of questionable virtue (called *lorettes*) who flocked to the quarter in search of wealthy husbands.

From the church I followed rue Bourdaloue to rue Saint-Lazare. Hughes's role model, French writer Alexandre Dumas, lived on this street in 1833. Dumas's grandmother was a black slave from Santo Domingo; Dumas was therefore *métis*, or mulatto. In his attempts to persuade his father to allow him to become a writer, Hughes had often referred to Dumas as the archetype of a successful black writer. But Hughes's father dismissed the idea, countering that Dumas was successful in Paris—where people did not care about skin color.

Hughes's father didn't get this quite right—the French did, and do, care about skin color. Dumas bore the brunt of racial slurs in his day. And during the 2002 presidential election in France, a vituperatively right-wing, anti-immigrant (which translates to anti–people of color) candidate came uncomfortably close to winning. But in my experience, France's brand of racism is not nearly as oppressive and overwhelming as that of the United States, and it is mixed with notions of nationality and class that make it a more complex subject to ponder.

From rue Saint-Lazare, I quickly arrived at its intersection with rue Notre-Dame-de-Lorette. This is the street that I believe Hughes took as he made his way toward "Black Montmartre." Soon after turning onto rue Notre-Dame-de-Lorette, I arrived at place Saint-Georges. Here, the beautiful Thiers library and the Théâtre Saint-Georges are among the establishments lining the square. The Thiers library is housed in a *hôtel particulier*, or private mansion, that was rebuilt after being totally destroyed during the 1870 uprising known as the Commune. It was reconstructed in the style of Louis XVI. By comparison, the trompe l'oeil façade of the theater is uninspiring. The centerpiece of the square is a statue of Gavarni, a nineteenth-century cartoonist who was fond of sketching the neighborhood *lorettes*.

After passing through place Saint-Georges, rue La Bruyère is the first street to the left. At its intersection with rue Pigalle was an establishment called the Flea Pit, a popular meeting place for African Americans. Like so many of the places that Hughes and other African Americans frequented during the between-war years, it no longer exists. And though I have searched, I have never been able to find a reference that gives the exact address of the Flea Pit. So whenever I am in the area, I always look at the Asian caterer, pharmacy, bakery, and restaurants on this corner and wonder where it might have been.

Rampersad writes that the Pit was where Hughes ended up on his first day. But from Hughes's account in *The Big Sea*, one might conclude that he went elsewhere—to a destination farther up rue Notre-Dame-de-Lorette, past its intersection with rue Pigalle. Another gathering place for African Americans was once located there.

Continuing up the street, I noted the Ethiopian restaurant Addis Abeba at Number 56—it has served the neighborhood for the past five years. Hughes loved Ethiopia, and wrote several poems about this East African country. I imagine that he would have been a frequent customer of this tastefully simple eatery, had it existed when he lived here. I couldn't resist stopping in for a serving of *ye berà wàt* (a spicy beef ragout accompanied by spinach, cabbage, and carrots; Ethiopian cheese; and a salad of lettuce, tomato, and onion atop spongy *injera*, a flat bread made from millet). It was delicious.

Upon reaching rue Pigalle, I walked to Number 52, the address of Le Grand Duc, one of the most popular nightclubs of Black

Montmartre. Sadly, it no longer exists—an Asian fast food shop called Miss China Lunch Box sits here now. Hughes worked here as a dishwasher for most of the six months that he was in Paris. The music he heard in the nightclub inspired Hughes to work jazz rhythms into his poetry. The "Duc" was also the nightclub in which he met Florence Jones and Bricktop, masterful entertainers who were the only two African-American women performing in Paris at that time. Looking up the street, one can see the same view of Sacré-Coeur that Hughes undoubtedly saw when he came to work at 11:00 P.M. and when he left at 7:00 A.M.

Not far from here is rue Fontaine, once the site of numerous jazz clubs. When Bricktop left Le Grand Duc, she opened her own club at Number 1 on the corner. She called it Bricktop's, and it quickly became a formidable rival to the Duc. As late as 1950, she owned several other nightspots in Paris.

At Number 5, rue Fontaine (now a restaurant called Le Théâtre de Don Carmelo), Eugene Bullard had a club called L'Escadrille. Bullard was a World War I veteran who fought under French command and became the first African-American fighter pilot. He owned or managed several businesses in Black Montmartre, and was manager of the Duc when Hughes worked there. Number 16, rue Fontaine, was the home of Zelli's, another club that was managed by Bullard. It is now a flower shop called Samantha Fleurs.

Many other nightspots were located on this block, as well—the Royal Montmartre, the Cotton Club, and the Tempo Club were among them. Today, small shops, bars, and restaurants line this thoroughly working-class street. There are also several theaters and cabarets—L'Abbé Constantin and the Bus Palladium at Number 6, the Théâtre Fontaine at Number 10 and the Nouvelle Eve at Number 25.

Chez Boudon, another popular hangout for black musicians in Hughes's time, was on the corner of rue Fontaine and rue de Douai. From what Hughes recounts in *The Big Sea*, this may be the club in which he made his first contact with African Americans in Montmartre when he arrived in 1924. He struck up a conversation with some musicians and inquired about finding a cheap hotel and job opportunities. One of them advised him to go to the hotel across the street to see if he could find a suitable room (likely the Hôtel Liseux, which was located at Number 24, rue Fontaine; this is now the address of the Pandora Station bar).

Hughes took a room for the night, but found the rates too high to stay there for the long term. He returned to Chez Boudon (or to the Pit, if you accept Rampersad's account) the following day, and had the good fortune to meet Sonya, a Russian dancer who was also down on her luck. She took him to a very cheap hotel, where Hughes paid for two weeks' lodging in advance. He thanked Sonya and left her to go to the Gare du Nord to pick up his bags. When he returned, he found that Sonya had moved into the room, which, she announced, they would be sharing! Soon afterward, she found a job at Zelli's that kept hunger at bay and a roof over their heads while Hughes searched for employment.

The Moloko Bar at Number 26, rue Fontaine, is located where Bricktop opened her last Paris club in 1950. Across the street at the café/bar Le Dépanneur (Number 27, rue Fontaine), I mused over the caricature of a black barman that was chosen to advertise this establishment. Perhaps it is an oblique reference to the history of African Americans in the quarter. Josephine Baker opened Chez Josephine farther up the street at Number 39 in 1926. It was the first of many nightclubs to bear her name.

At the end of rue Fontaine, across from place Blanche, the famous cabaret Moulin Rouge still stands. Hughes and his ladylove, Anne Marie Coussey (called Mary in his autobiography), danced there in the spring of 1924. Lena Horne performed here during the 1950s, and African-American artist Loïs Mailou Jones captured the cabaret's image in a painting in 1955.

Black performers have been enthusiastically received here since the 1920s. Dancer Harry Fleming performed here in 1927, and the musical *Blackbirds* enjoyed tremendous success in 1929. *Blackbirds* featured an all-star cast of 100 black artists, including Adelaide Hall, Bill Robinson, Aida Ward, Tim Moore, the Blackbirds Beauty Chorus, the world-famous Plantation Orchestra, and Johnny Hudgins.

In 1989, Ella Fitzgerald, Barbara Hendricks, and Ray Charles performed at the Moulin Rouge to commemorate the 100th anniversary of this music hall. And in 1995, African-American opera singer Jessye Norman and French singer Charles Aznavour participated in the launching of the Lancôme perfume "Poême" by giving a private performance here. I enjoyed perusing the holograms in the entryway that highlight the history of this classic Paris music hall.

Leaving the Moulin Rouge, I walked to the corner of boulevard de Clichy and rue Lepic. Hughes states that he and Sonya walked up rue Lepic as she led him to the hotel that they would call home. The slope of the street looks gentle from this vantage point, but becomes steeper as you walk its length. I turned left onto rue Lepic, noting the incongruous façade of the Häagen-Dazs ice cream parlor across the street. Josephine Baker opened a water valve and flooded this street to cool off the set of the 1934 film *Zouzou*, in which she was starring.

Proceeding up the hill, I encountered the Tabac des 2 Moulins at Number 15. This café is where Amélie worked in *Amélie*. I continued climbing, following rue Lepic as it turned sharply left and then traced a long semicircular path to the right along the slope of the hill. The hustle and bustle of human traffic in front of storefronts and cafés near the boulevard de Clichy gave way to a peaceful, more residential neighborhood. A poster in the window of the restaurant Au Virage Lepic at Number 61 depicts Josephine Baker in her famous banana skirt.

The Moulin de la Galette, one of the last remaining windmills in Paris, sits atop a hill to the north of rue Lepic. In the spring and summer, the wisteria blossoms on the trees make a pretty picture here. It is a beautiful oasis of greenery in this city of limestone and gypsum walls. Several art galleries and restaurants line the south side of the road on the next stretch of rue Lepic. Arriving at place Jean-Baptiste Clément, I admired the large private residences behind the stone walls on the north side of the street. These homes and those located behind wrought iron gates on the south side of the square are reminders that some Parisians are lucky enough to live in single-family dwellings. Place Jean-Baptiste Clément is a delightful area where one can stop, sit down, and soak in the atmosphere of this bucolic *quartier*.

Past place Jean-Baptiste Clément I reached rue Norvins, where the tranquility dissipated as I entered the part of Montmartre that draws the most tourists. I followed rue Norvins to the place du Tertre, where I saw the perpetual tangle of umbrellas and tourist-filled restaurants. Once cluttered with caricaturists, only serious artists are permitted to work here now. Hughes wrote that this was where he and Coussey had their last meal together before she was forced to return to England. (Her father had refused to continue her monthly allowance, and she could no longer afford to stay in Paris.)

Descending the steep stairs of rue Chappe on the south side of Montmartre, I found my way to rue des Trois Frères. This was the last street Hughes lived on before he left Paris. Long ago, it formed the boundary of the seventeenth-century Abbey of Montmartre (a replacement for the original abbey built by Louis VI farther up the hill during the twelfth century). Alain Locke (African-American educator, Rhodes scholar, and author of *The New Negro*) visited Hughes in his attic apartment on rue des Trois Frères in July 1924.

Walking up the right-hand side of the street, I noted the Afro-Antillean restaurant Douceurs Caraïbes at Number 18 and the Brazilian restaurant Carajas at Number 24. One could easily suppose that Hughes would have appreciated having such establishments so close to home, particularly since their prices are quite reasonable. But they did not exist when he lived here. Both places are small and intimate. Douceurs Caraïbes offers traditional African and Caribbean dishes such as *colombo* (goat, chicken, or pork) and beef *maffé*, while Carajas proudly serves Brazil's national dish, *feijoada* (pork, black beans, cabbage, and manioc flour), alongside many others. Carajas has a particularly inviting decor, with vivid tablecloths bearing images of the sea and musical instruments—used for Brazil's martial art w and its pre-Lenten *Carnaval* celebration—adorning the walls.

Because neither Hughes nor Rampersad cites a street number for his last home in Paris, I could only look at the uninspired façades along this curved street and guess where Hughes might have stayed. I walked past the grocer Chez Ali (called Maison Collignon in the film *Amélie*—Amélie lived above it) and continued to the end of the street just below the place Emile Goudeau. Here, to the south, there is another magnificent view of Paris.

I took a few moments to mount the stairs of the square to see the Bateau Lavoir at 11 bis. A recently installed exhibit in the window gives the names of the artists and poets who once lived here, including Picasso and Modigliani. There are also photos, sketches, and text (in English and in French) that provide an overview of the site's history as well as information on the Musée de Montmartre.

The Bateau Lavoir was the studio in which Picasso painted *Les Demoiselles d'Avignon* (1907), his first Cubist painting and the first to reflect the influence that African art wielded on this artistic genius. I wondered what Hughes thought of this painting, and whether or not he ever had the chance to meet Picasso (whose work was on the cover of the Italian translation of *The Big Sea*).

The literary references that pertain to Hughes's life on this historic hill end here, so I descended the steps below the square and proceeded down rue Ravignan, then to the place des Abbesses, which harbors the leafy square Jehan-Rictus. I entered the square to gaze at the blue-tiled "I Love You" wall, where multilingual declarations of love are exhibited, and thought once more about how Hughes and Coussey meandered down the hill from place du Tertre after their last dinner together. Might they have strayed into this romantic spot? I reflected for a moment before returning to the bustling world outside.

André

Alice Kaplan

I met André at the first party of the year in Pau, where our junior-year-abroad group had a six-week orientation before settling down in Bordeaux. He came bounding into the room at me. He was long and wiry with shiny black hair and a devil smile on his face. He sat me down on the couch, put one hand on each of my shoulders: "Alors, ma petite américaine, tu t'appelles comment?" The room was packed with noisy foreign students. André's voice drowned them out completely. "Serre-moi," he said, taking his arms off my shoulders and holding them out toward me. I didn't know those words in French but I figured out exactly what they meant from André's body: "Serre-moi" meant "hold me." Ten minutes later I went with him into the nearest bedroom—I was in love with my own recklessness—and he put his shirt on a lamp for just the right amount of light. We got into bed and his shirt caught on fire. It was like that with him, sudden blazes; he was always jumping up to put out some fire or other, leaping and howling at his own antics. His main activities were mountain climbing (the Pyrenees), painting, and chasing women. He was twenty-seven and he worked for a graphic arts firm, but it was impossible to think of him as an office worker.

I used to wait for him to come into the café around seven. He entered the room like a mannequin, one shoulder slightly behind the other and his legs in front of him. His smile was subtle and controlled; no teeth showed. He had a way of stopping to survey the room before coming over to my table that made me hold my breath for fear he wouldn't come. He looked down his greyhound nose at each of my girlfriends, bent his long frame forward to give the ceremonial kiss on each cheek, all around the table. I was last. I got four kisses, two on each cheek, with the same geometric precision.

I liked to watch André sitting across from me at the café, smoking his cigarette with his head tilted to one side to show off his cheek bones. He exuded an Egyptian beauty, his jet black hair bouncing off his shoulders, his long muscles showing through his skin. There was so much energy in that body, it seemed to be in motion even when he was sitting.

He was a moralist and he had theories. He talked about his "aesthetic folly"—his drunken outings—and about "the bourgeois complacency" of most women (their desire for commitment and stability; his love of freedom). He thought American women talked too much, but he liked me because I was natural. Although I shouldn't wear so much black.

I kept a diary and I started taking notes on André: "André ate a dead bee he found on the steps of a church." I liked to watch him. I studied André showering. He scrubbed every inch of himself with a soapy washcloth that he wrapped around his hand like an envelope. I watched him washing all his muscles under the soap, especially the ones around his chest he'd got from climbing mountains. I thought to myself, this is the way a man showers when he only gets a shower once a week. I thought of all the men I knew who showered every day, sloppily, and who had nothing to wash off.

I went to classes, part of our six-week orientation to French culture. In class I spent a lot of time with my head on the desk, nothing but André in it. I went to the language lab for phonetic testing and they said I was starting to get the regional Gascon accent in my "r"s, I should watch out. I had been studying André too hard.

We read André Bazin and learned the difference between Hollywood film and the French *cinéma d'auteur*, film so marked by the style of its director you can say it has an author, like a book. One day we were all bused to the Casino in Pau, to watch Alain Resnais and Marguerite Duras's *Hiroshima mon amour* on a big screen. The movie begins with lovers, a French actress and a Japanese architect. In the first frames, you see their bodies close up, their sweat mixed with shiny sprinkles that look like ash—the ash of the atomic bomb in Hiroshima. I watched their bodies and I heard their voices. The dialogue is sparse in this movie, the sentences are as simple as sentences in a first-year language text, except that they are erotic. One staccato statement after another, the pronoun "tu"—the familiar "you"—in every sentence. The movie taught me what "tu" means, how intimate, how precious—"You are like a thousand women together," he says, and she: "That is because you don't know me." The sentences are so bare that they seem to mean everything—a thousand sentences packed together in a few words, every sentence an unexploded bomb. She: "You speak French well." He: "Don't I. I'm happy you've finally noticed" (laughter). After it was over, I still felt inside the bare secret world of the movie and went to sit in a park, where I wrote to André in an erotic trance. "When I lose my words in French," I wrote, "a radical transformation occurs. My thoughts are no longer thoughts, they are images, visions. More important—the feeling of power in not being able to communicate, the feeling of being stripped down to the most fundamental communication. I am with you, I see black and then flashes: a leg, a sex, a nose. Seen, felt, tasted. The taste of your body pursues me," I wrote. "Like an essence."

But André wasn't buying it. I still have the letter, stuck between the pages of my diary from that year; it has his corrections all over it. Where I wrote "la joie de la reverse," which is made-up French for "the joy of reversal," he crossed it out and wrote "the joy of anti-conformism." (One of his slogans about himself was that he was an anti-conformist.)

This should have been my first clue that what I really wanted from André was language, but in the short run all it did was make me feel more attached to him, without knowing why I was attached. I can still hear the sound he made when he read my love letter: "T,t,t," with that little ticking sound French people make by putting the tips of their tongues on the roof of their mouths—a fussy, condescending sound, by way of saying, "that's *not* how one says it." What I wanted more than anything, more than André even, was to make those sounds, which were the true sounds of being French, and so even as he was insulting me and discounting my passion with a vocabulary lesson, I was listening and studying and recording his response.

He decided to take me out for a ninety-six-franc meal, for my education. *Tripes à la mode de Caen*—the stomach of some animal, and the *spécialité de la maison*. I ate it in huge bites, to show him I wasn't squeamish. Before he had too much to drink he made a speech at me, in his high moral style: "You represent the woman I would like to love if I were older and if I dominated myself. I am very happy to have known you. But I want a woman I can express myself with. You understand my words but not my language—you don't even realize how great a problem it is between us." (I wrote the whole speech down in my diary afterwards, word for word.) He tried to pronounce the difference between "word" and "world" in English—he thought it was funny they were so alike, and that their similarity had to do with us, with our problem. He couldn't make the "l" sound in "world." He ordered schnapps for two plus a cognac, then another. He drank them all. We raced off to a disco in his Deux Chevaux. He leaped out under the strobe lights, out of my sight. I stood outside the dancing *piste* and watched him sidle up to four different women, one after another, twirling each of them around him in his own athletic interpretation of "le rock." His sister was at the discothèque. She advised me to grab him and start making out with him if I wanted to get home. Twice on the way home he stopped the car to weep in my lap, sobbing giant tears.

The next day I got a note that said: "I'm sorry Alice. Hier soir j'avais trop bu. J'espère que tu ne m'en tiendras pas rigueur. Tendresse. André." Which means: "I drank too much last night. Don't be too hard on me." I received this note like a haiku and pasted it in my diary.

That week I kept running over his speech in my mind. What was the difference between his words and my words, his world and my world? When I said a French word, why wasn't it the same as when he said one? When I said a French word, why wasn't it the same as when he said one? What could I do to make it be the same? I had to stick it out with him, he was transmitting new words to me every day and I needed more. In fact, while Barbara and Buffy and Kacy (André dubbed us "l'équipe"—the team) rolled their eyes about what a raw deal I was getting from this creep, I was all the more determined to be with him. He was in all my daydreams now. I wanted to crawl into his skin, live in his body, be him. The words he used to talk to me, I wanted to use back. I wanted them to be my words.

The last weekend I spent with André, we went to a sleazy hotel in Toulouse. He was on another drinking binge and we both got bitten up by bedbugs—or so I thought at the time. When I got back to the dorm my neck was swollen and my ear was all red. I was hot, and I went into a long sleep that I thought was due to exhaustion from being with André. Within forty-eight hours the swelling on my neck felt like a tumor and the whole side of my face was swollen. My right eye was shut. I hid in my dorm room. When I had to go for a meal I wrapped my neck in a scarf and put a hat down over my right eye. I was almost too sick to care that André was spending the night down the hall from me with Maïté, a French woman who was one of the assistants in charge of orienting us. She was part Basque, like him, and lanky like him, only softer; she dressed in Indian prints and sheepskin vests.

The doctors didn't really know what was wrong with me, so they did tests. They tried one medicine, then another. Finally they sent me to a convent, where I got free antibiotic shots in my behind daily. I went there every day for seven days to get rid of the infection. The stark white cot where I submitted to the treatment, the nuns' quiet efficiency, had a soothing effect on me. I was cleansed by charity.

When I came out of the worst of my sickness I thought about it like this: it was the two of them against me. Two people who had the words and shared the world and were busy communicating in their authentic language, and me, all alone in my room. Maïté had something I couldn't have, her blood and her tongue and a name with accents in it. I was burning with race envy.

I spent a lot of time reading, and sitting in cafés with "l'équipe," my team of girlfriends, and writing in my diary about André and what he meant. He wanted me to be natural, and I wanted him to make me French. When I thought back on the way the right side of me had swelled up, my neck and my ear and my eye, it was as if half of my face had been at war with that project. Half of me, at least, was allergic to André.

The day our group left for Bordeaux, André and Maïté were standing together at the bus stop and André gave me the ceremonial cheek kiss right in front of her, and whispered the possibility of a visit in my tender but healed ear. I could count on his infidelity working both ways.

In Bordeaux we signed up for housing with Monsieur Garcia, the administrative assistant of the University of California program. "You can live with a family or you can have liberty," Garcia said. A family meant nice quarters and no visitors; liberty meant scruffier quarters. Everyone knew that liberty really meant liberty to have sex, and life in France without sex was inconceivable to me.

André showed up in Bordeaux two or three times that year, strictly on the run. Once he claimed he was in town doing a two-week *stage* (the French term for a mini-apprenticeship) on bug extermination with his friend Serge. He rang the doorbell in the middle of the night and leapt into my bed. His breath smelled like rotten fruit and he had one of those stubborn erections that doesn't even respond to sex. Finally he rolled away from me, muttering what I thought was "Je suis costaud" (I'm strong), falling into a dead sleep. After a few days of thinking about the phonetic possibilities ("choo-ee co stow" or "choo-ee co stew"?), and looking through dictionaries, I decided he had actually been saying, "je suis encore saoul" (I'm still drunk), only drunkenly: "j'suis 'co soo," as a way of explaining why he hadn't been able to come. I was still putting up with André, for his beauty and for his words.

Each room in my boardinghouse had a sink and bidet. Outside was the outhouse, with maggots. The other boarders were immigrant workers. Across the hall was Caméra, from the République of Guinée, who had a job in construction and was trying to study math on the side with do-it-yourself tapes. He helped me set up a *camping gaz* so I could make omelettes. He took me to the African Student Association dance where I started dancing with the biggest creep there. "Il ne vaut rien," Caméra warned me, "he's worth nothing; a first-rate hustler." The hustler danced like a wild marionette and told me what he liked: "fun, acid, women, music." I made a rendezvous with him, which I didn't keep. Caméra was angry with me, and we stopped speaking.

For weeks I didn't want to open the door of my room, for fear of seeing Caméra, his disapproving glance. I kept the door to my room closed, as though some father had grounded me. When I was out I had the energy of an escaped convict; when I was home the righteousness of a cloistered nun. It felt familiar.

I had to go to the bathroom all the time. The more I dreaded the outhouse, the more I had to go. I planned outings to cafés, to use the bathrooms there. I knew which cafés in my part of town had clean bathrooms, with seats, and which ones had stand-up Turkish toilets.

If I timed it right I could go to the best café in town, the Régent, anesthetize myself with steamed milk, go to the bathroom, and make it home for a night of dreams. When I walked home from the café it was pitch black and sometimes a *clochard*, a bum, yelled obscenities at me. I was too lost in my thoughts to be scared.

The room became my world. Clean sheets once a week. I began to recognize the people on my street: the man with no arms, the *tabac* lady with the patchwork shawl, the old concierge and his creaking keys, and Papillon, the pharmacist around the corner. My room and I were together now; night and morning rituals established themselves with pleasantly passing weeks. The bidet was no longer exotic; I soaked my tired feet in it. I had a wool shawl that I wrapped around my nightgowned shoulders and that transported me into timelessness. I put the shawl on to read: *Le Père Goriot*, about a nineteenth-century boardinghouse, and *Les Liasons dangereuses*, about a woman who controls her world through letters but is destroyed in the end. My room could exist in any century, in any French city.

The administration of the California program arranged all kinds of outings and connections for us students. I babysat for a rich family who lived in a modern house. Their floor was made of polished stones. I was invited to a chateau and I wore my best dress, ready to discuss literature. I got there and my French hosts greeted me in sneakers. They were growing Silver Queen corn in their backyard, and they wanted a fourth for tennis. Of all the Americans in my group the one they liked best was the freckled jock who could hardly

speak French and went everywhere on his ten-speed bike. I was wait-
ing to be rewarded for my good French, but he got all the attention.
He was having fun playing the American mascot, while I was doing
all the hard work of learning their language and what I thought were
their social customs. I would have been ready to pose as the
Marlboro Man to get the kind of attention he got from the French.
But I had veered off in the other direction; I was trying to be French.
Besides, I knew his ploy wouldn't work for me: a girl can't be a
Marlboro Man.

I was always watching and pretending, pretending and watching. I met a guy from Colorado. We were sitting at the French
student restaurant together and I was peeling my pear so carefully,
he said, he didn't know I was American. We went to the French student restaurant to meet people but no one spoke at the table, just
peeled their fruit and left. This guy (his name is gone) and I made
up stories instead of going to bed together (we weren't supposed
to go to bed with each other: we were on our junior year abroad).
In one, I would be a prostitute who specialized in American men
wanting to meet French girls. The joke would be that I wouldn't be
French at all. We figured out where I would have to go and what I
would wear and say, and what they would say. He would be my
proxynète, the entrepreneur, and we would make tons of money and
live well.

He went off and found a French girlfriend, a real one, and the
next time I saw him they were on his moped, her arms around his
waist, her hair in one of those high French pony tails waving in the

breeze. When he saw me he waved proudly, a little sheepish to have me see him like that in the middle of his fantasy. I waved back and laughed.

I wanted to travel on my own, be brave, but I wasn't. I was always afraid of making a *faux pas*. I took a taxi to the train station to catch a train and I opened the taxi door just as a car was racing down the street. The car smashed into the taxi door, crumpling it. It was a fancy taxi, a top-of-the-line Renault, and the driver was screaming at me about his insurance and how much my foreigner stupidity was going to cost him. He was so disgusted he wouldn't let me pay the fare. I skulked into the station, my head hung low: this was my great adventure.

In the seventeen years since I met André, my ear has swelled up on me from time to time, although never as dramatically as that September in Pau. When I was writing this book, it happened again. The swelling came on so quickly that I went right to the doctor, who took one look at me and said, "You have herpes simplex on your ear." He'd only seen one case of herpes on the ear in all his years of medical practice: a man who had the cold sore on his mouth kissed his wife on the ear, and she got the virus.

As I searched back in my mind, I could see the tiny little blister on André's upper lip, a neat imperfection I was determined to ignore but that turned into his legacy. My precious ear, my radar, my antenna: the locus of my whole attraction to French, and André went right for it! Maybe he bit me there, maybe he kissed me, or maybe he just whispered some of his words with his lip up against my earlobe, and the virus took.

At the time, when I thought about him and Maïté, I thought, "It's because my French isn't good enough" and "It's because she's French." When he told me I couldn't understand his language, André had picked the accusation I was most vulnerable to. Afterwards I thought, "I'll show him. I'll know all there is to know about his language. I'll know his language better than he does, someday."

After I had become a French professor, I wrote André, and he wrote back. The nonconformist was still living at the same address, and I had moved ten times. I felt glad about that. There were a few spelling mistakes in his letter to me, the kind I'm hired to correct. But I didn't feel gleeful about his spelling, because it hadn't been spelling that I wanted from him. I wanted to breathe in French with André, I wanted to sweat French sweat. It was the rhythm and pulse of his French I wanted, the body of it, and he refused me, he told me I could never get that. I had to get it another way.

Foie Gras Dreams

Melinda Bergman Burgener

It is forty-five minutes until dinner. My husband, Arnold, and I are
standing ankle-deep in French muck—beige and runny like potter's
slip-glaze, but startlingly acrid to our noses—confronting a moral
dilemma. Our host, Madame Etchegoyan, has just removed her feeding funnel from duck number thirteen. She is persuading her flock to
turn their brown, normal-size livers into pale, engorged, exquisite-
tasting giants—the very same ambrosial, melt-in-the-mouth foie gras
we had sampled at her dinner table the evening before.

We had arrived, unannounced, at 6:00 P.M. looking for lodgings
outside the dot-size Basque town of Arhansus. Unruffled, Mme.
Etchegoyan had shown us a room on the first floor, at the back of
her large farmhouse, then asked us not whether we wanted dinner,
but at what time. We liked her at once; here was a woman who

understood from our ravenous but droopy appearance that we needed large quantities of good food but didn't want to go searching for it. She wanted only to verify our foreign palates: *Foie gras? Garbure? Confit?* A *oui* to each segued into a guessing game—were we: *Anglais? Allemands? Irlandais?* Her teenage son suggested *Australiens?* Then they ran out of countries. *Américains*, it seemed, had never visited this remote spot in the Pyrenees before. Astonished but delighted, she welcomed us into her home.

At the family dinner, we were launched into gastronomic heaven with the first sublime morsel of fattened duck liver. It was difficult, even with faltering French and full mouths, to curtail our praise. Monsieur Etchegoyan beamed and boasted, *"Maison fait!"*—made right there, by Madame. We quit raving about the foie gras only long enough to devour the rest of the meal: rich regional vegetable soup, preserved duck with tiny fried potatoes, baby garden salad, farm cheese, crepes; everything *maison fait*, everything delicious.

While we stuffed ourselves, we fielded questions about hamburgers and handguns and asked our own about foie gras making. How was it done? How could anything as common as a duck's liver taste this exalted? Their vague responses succeeded only in conjuring up visions of Madame E. endlessly dipping into her apron and broadcasting zillions of handfuls of corn to exceptionally hungry, exceedingly lucky ducks.

Dinner was over at midnight, and within minutes, with bellies bursting, we were asleep in our room facing the chicken coops. But the fowl noises and smells must have contaminated some echoing snippets of our mealtime conversation, producing a vivid and unsettling dream. I saw my own mother—her Bronx accent eerily French—metamorphosed into a Basque harridan who nudged and crammed her skinny ducklings with more food than they could possibly hold. She began softly, with coaxing, clucking noises. When that failed, she cried out—how often I'd heard this—"Babies are starving all over the world and you do not like my cooking?" This guilt trip worked magic on the dream ducks, just as it had on me: Willingly, they ate and they ate until their little livers puffed and ballooned and began to explode, like dried corn in a hot pan. With relief, I opened my eyes. I smiled when I heard the chickens clucking and pecking outside our windows.

The following morning, Monsieur E., his teenage son, and his farmer brother joined us at the breakfast table. Innocently, we opted for the same meal the men were served daily—an option that has since replaced the word "continental" with "monumental" whenever I think of French breakfasts. We each ate a fried farm egg, house-made Bayonne ham (rubbed with local peppers from nearby Espelette), house-cured bacon, and an entire baguette (which the Basques held against their chests to slice). A carafe of strong coffee was placed between my husband and me, alongside a juice pitcher of boiled raw milk. The men also had large pitchers in front of them, but these contained red wine—which they polished off, one juice glass at a time.

Madame E. took only tea. Finished with her morning chores, she sat with us and talked foie gras. We learned she fed sixty ducks at a time during a two-week fattening process. The feed, 100 kilos (220 pounds) of corn and one cup of salt, was pressure-cooked, by her—

maison fait again!—every morning. Methodically, the daily feedings were increased: ten ounces, morning and evening, on day one; three and one-third pounds, morning and evening, by day fourteen. What appetites these birds had! Curiosity overpowering us, we finally asked to watch how this sublime *delicacy* was achieved. Madame, to our surprise, looked reluctant, but Monsieur beamed once more and complimented me on my use of precisely the right word. He said, yes, it was the *delicacy* of Madame's touch in feeding the ducks that made them eat much more than others—himself included—could persuade them to.

I surveyed our breakfast plates and worried for our own livers; were we incubating two more sitting ducks for Madame E.'s rich foods and delicate insistence?

Arrangements were made to observe that evening's feeding. We arrived in the duck barn promptly at 7:00 P.M. From a waist-high open platform divided into two back-to-back rows of thirty individual wire cages, sixty duck heads protruded. On the floor, under each animal, was a mountain of putty-like guano almost reaching the cage. The smell was revolting. Madame E., garbed in a large plastic apron, had just begun, but was already splattered—face, arms, apron—with streaks of this putty. An overhead track ran the length of the platform; attached to it, dangling from a bungee-like cord, was a feeding funnel with an eighteen-inch shaft. Madame E. grabbed a duck's head and deftly inserted the tube into the open beak in one double-quick move. The end of the spout was somewhere deep inside the bird. She plopped a huge amount of feed—it was almost day fourteen—into the cone, then hit a switch. The funnel vibrated noisily as the food was mechanically pushed through it, into the duck's gut. When the tube was removed, the animal was dazed, immobilized, barely alive. I thought, "What nasty business I'm watching." My face must have reflected this, for Madame looked up and quietly said, "*C'est méchant, non?*" Then she moved delicately down the line.

A duck is four months old at the end of this frenzy, at which time Madame E. inserts a kitchen knife into the beak and slits the roof of the mouth. She removes each liver, keeps it and the bird on ice, hoses and disinfects the barn, and personally delivers her product. The grossly enlarged creamy-yellow liver weighs between one and almost two pounds and will grace some of the region's finest menus.

Foie gras is the supreme fruit of gastronomy, and Madame E. produces the choicest fruit on the vine. She keeps only ten livers—but as many as sixty ducks—a year for family eating. The livers are too dear to withhold more; their tasty incubators are more affordable. The following day she would usher sixty new birds into her barn.

In the fantasies of a foolish, squeamish American, foie gras making was a Walt Disney production with folksy overtones. The reality is harsh. But delicate Madame E. understands her business very well; a farmer's life just doesn't happen to be a dream.

She moved down the line. We left the barn to prepare for dinner.

Liberté

Valerie J. Brooks

I'm finally here, in the City of Light, a city I long ago called "the city of my imagination," as if that's where it would always remain. But here I am, actually standing on French soil, outside Charles de Gaulle Airport, French francs in my purse, the smell of strong French cigarettes drifting past my nose. A Frenchman next to me carries a bouquet of flowers that gives off the scent of spring. All of this should excite my romantic expectations of France, but as my husband and I climb onto a shuttle bus, headed to our hotel on the Left Bank, I suddenly wish I were back home. Dan says, "Are you OK? You're here, you're finally here." He has made my dream come true, given me the gift of Paris for my birthday. I nod and say, "Yes, I'm OK," but I'm not. I can't explain. Not to him; not even to myself.

We are caught in rush hour on the freeway, passing sound walls—some covered in graffiti, others made of a beautiful cinder-block design and latticed wood. As Renaults, Peugeots, and scooters scream by at alarming speeds, I try to find this notorious traffic charming, oh so Parisian. Instead I lean my forehead against the window and wonder if this whole Paris obsession has been a mistake, if I should have left it as it was—an idea, an escape hatch for the times I felt imprisoned in someone else's idea of what I should be.

I ask the driver to let us off at the Arc de Triomphe, and Dan looks at me as if I'm crazy, then shrugs and smiles—he thinks I know what I'm doing. In fact, I don't. At the Arc we join the masses. Dan looks up and says, "It's huge."

I'm pleased by his awe. I want this trip to be as important for him as it is for me. Then, after explaining that Napoleon ordered the Arc to be built in honor of his soldiers after the Battle of Austerlitz, I cross my arms and shake my head. The first famous site I've chosen to see is a war memorial—not an auspicious start for the likes of me, but something my father would have appreciated. Then I remember that he actually stood right here, where I am standing now.

When I was a teen, I found photos of him taken during World War II in his officer's uniform, including one of him standing on the Champs Elysées with the Arc in the background. Hoping to find something in common with him, I had showed him the photo album and said, "You were in Paris!"

"I was an officer under Eisenhower," he said. "We marched into Paris on V-E Day."

Wanting more, I said, "I just love France."

My father's face congealed. "The French are cowards," he said. "They surrendered to Hitler to keep Paris from being bombed." I had no idea how to respond to this. "London was almost bombed to the ground," he continued, as if this explained his position. "That," he said, "is why the English have every right to hate the French."

I turn to Dan and say, "Feel like walking?" He does. After traveling all the way from Oregon and sitting for almost thirteen hours on planes, I think stretching our legs is probably a good idea. We move to the sidewalk, rolling our carry-ons behind us. My father's 1944 photos show an almost naked avenue, but now shops and mature trees line it as far as the eye can see.

"What's the matter?" Dan asks. In the nineteen years we've been together, he's developed a seismograph that measures my inner disturbances. I force a smile and say, "French fashion! Oh, God, look at those." We stand in front of a boutique where the adult clothes are so small, they look as if they are made for children.

Dan says, "Want me to buy you something? How about that dress?" He points to a sophisticated little black thing, and I laugh, take his arm, and say, "I love you," without explaining I would need two of those stitched together, and we'd never be able to afford even one. "I'm here to see art and soak up the *joie de vivre*," I say, then kiss his cheek to hide my growing uneasiness, thinking maybe I'm just suffering from jet lag.

After stopping for tea and resting our legs, we finally arrive at our hotel, the Bellechasse, in the heart of Saint-Germain-des-Prés. We're exhausted as we sign in, then squeeze into the phone-booth-size elevator. "I swear, no matter how hard or soft the mattress," I say, "I'm going to sleep like the dead."

Dan says, "Did you know that we were over a mile from our hotel when you asked if I wanted to walk?" In our room, he flops down on the bed and within minutes falls into an enviable deep sleep. I'm exhausted, but I can't quiet my mind, so I sit on the windowsill looking into a courtyard, listening to the evening sounds of tinkling dishes and traffic, wondering where my father spent his first night in Paris and trying to imagine what it must have felt like to liberate this city.

I'm softly humming and stop for a moment to identify the tune. It's a song from an album by Françoise Hardy, the French *yé-yé* girl. I was fourteen when I won her album in a radio contest. I had never heard of her at the time. The album, *The Essential and the Existential*, was all in French. I had tossed it on my desk with no intention of ever listening to it. But the cover was so bright red it pulsed, and I picked it up again.

As I stared at the album, a close-up of a woman's face emerged, the type of face I'd been drawing for years. I peeled off the cellophane and put the album on my phonograph, and at the first sound of her voice, something in me I'd been struggling to find, something necessary and important, was given permission to breathe. The language soothed me like poetry.

Now that I'm finally in Paris, I think it only fitting to sing her song, which I begin. "*Voilà, je regarde les autres. Pourtant je ne leur trouve rien—*"

I'm interrupted by a French couple two rooms down who begin yelling at each other, starting a quarrel that will last for over half an hour. They slam doors; she cries; he pummels her with questions; she pleads with him, but he is relentless. This quarrel should be heated, romantic—but it's not. This quarrel is about power, not love. I'm shaking and close the window.

The couple finally stops, and I lie down next to Dan. But my body, like a tuning fork, holds the pitch of their fight, and a memory washes over me like an undertow, dragging me back to where I came from.

It was around the same time I won the album, the same time of year as now, May, just before Memorial Day. I was in the bathroom, pinning back my bangs with bobby pins, bangs that my father threatened to cut if he found them hanging in my eyes. My parents' American Legion uniforms hung from the bathtub rod, fresh from the dry cleaners—my mother's blue wool cape with gold lining, her white dress and white garrison cap; my father's dress blues with white shoulder cord and white belt. I didn't want to march in the parade, but as an American Legion Junior Auxiliary member, I was expected to. What I wanted was to wear heavy eyeliner like Françoise. I wanted to be sexy, thin, and mysterious, not just a straight-A student who was called "a sweet kid" by my classmates, "a smart girl" by parents and teachers, and "Crisco fat in the can" by the boy across the street.

When my parents' car pulled into the garage, I headed down the hall to meet Mom so I could help make supper. When Dad saw me, he put down his lunch bucket and walked toward me. I reached up. My bobby pins had fallen out.

"What's this?" he said, pointing at my bangs. "What did I tell you?"

"I'm not cutting my bangs," I said, the words slipping out before I could stop them.

His hand came up to slap my face. I ducked, missing his hand, and when I saw his expression, I ran to my room, where he caught up with me and threw me on the bed, trying to spank me as if I were a three-year-old. I pushed and kicked, yelling at him to stop. My mom was yelling at us both. Then I kicked hard. He let out a muffled groan and backed away, the color draining from his face. Mom led him away to their room across the hall. I jumped up and stood there, too scared to cry, sick over what I had done. I walked into the bathroom, closed the door, and cut my bangs.

After dinner, I was sitting on the couch, sketching a face, a girl with long straight hair and bangs, when my father walked by. I tensed as he stopped next to my chair. He said, "She looks just like you." I bit my lip, the kindness in his voice something I hadn't heard in a long time. Then he said, "But she looks so sad."

To this day I don't understand what happened between us, why the kindness crept back into my Dad's voice after we had hurt each other. I rub my eyes, then stare into the darkness of our hotel room, resisting the impulse to wake Dan and tell him what I have remembered. I slip into bed, and, just before I fall asleep, I hear the bells of Notre Dame.

The next morning, we eat a bountiful breakfast at the hotel surrounded by Chinese tourists, but I don't tell Dan about my recaptured memory of my father. In the light of a clear spring day, I want to make discoveries with a fresh palette, not color them with the past. Out on the rue de Bellechasse, we walk two blocks to the Musée d'Orsay, where I spend half the day feasting on impressionists and postimpressionists. Dan explores the decorative arts and furniture. After lunch, we find a neighborhood bar, Le Penalty, and I'm almost feeling exuberant about Paris when sirens sound—not just one police car, but a flotilla of cars and black buses that scream down the boulevard St. Germain. We finish our beers and walk out into the street. Along St. Germain, riot squads pour out of the buses and form a line, figures dressed in gray riot gear from head to foot, carrying curved rectangular gray shields. They face striking Metro workers, who shout their demands through megaphones and microphones. The riot squad remains tense while the workers inch their way across the street.

I hold my breath, recalling the Paris riots of May 1968, when French students occupied the Sorbonne, demanding better study conditions and an overhaul of traditional values and institutions. The unions joined their fight. Paris was shut down. Back then, I was near the end of my junior year in high school, and I rallied my fellow students and organized our own strike—the school board was refusing to fund new textbooks, and ours were being held together by duct tape; some had no covers, and our math books dated to the

1940s. My father, a school board member, discovered I had instigated the strike, and I was grounded for a month.

In protest, I would not join dinner conversations. My parents were active in New Hampshire primary activities, and dinner was full of political discussion. New Englanders talk politics the way some people talk sports. But I held my tongue and dreamed of being in Paris, smoking cigarettes in a café, talking politics with people who understood me. Then at dinner one evening my father said, "Too bad they can't get rid of Bobby Kennedy like they did his brother." I couldn't sleep that night.

I am lost in my thoughts when Dan takes my hand and says, "Let's get out of here before something happens." We leave and walk to the Jardin du Luxembourg, where we sit in the garden and watch people sail their miniature boats on the pond. Dan asks, "What's next on the agenda?" I take two aspirin and wonder why at every turn I'm reminded of my father, while Dan blissfully takes in the sights. I'm the one who should be amazed and awed. I'm the one who wanted so badly to feel part of this city. Instead, I feel oppressed.

That night we wander the streets and pass a restaurant where locals are eating mussels that smell so savory, I have to stop. Dan has *steak frites*. Then we drink cafés au lait at the Napoleon and find enough to divert ourselves that we don't have to talk about why I'm so unhappy.

The next morning, my spirits revive when we head for the expat hangouts of the 1920s literary set. During my twenties, I supported myself as an artist, and now that I'm a writer, I want to catch whatever remnants of that literary fever still linger. We head for the heart of Montparnasse and find the buildings where Gertrude Stein and Ezra Pound lived and where the Jockey Club used to be. At the Jockey, Kiki, the infamous artist's model, used to sing barracks songs to the accompaniment of a piano-playing cowboy, and Josephine Baker danced all night, dressed only in a black fur coat. At Hemingway's favorite café, La Closerie des Lilas, we order *cafés crèmes*, then head off to the busy intersection called Carrefour Vavin, the center of expat life in the twenties. We café-hop—the Rotonde, the Dôme, the Select—then end at the Dingo Bar, now the Auberge du Centre, where Hemingway met Fitzgerald.

At the Dingo, Dan says, "I think I need a break."

Jet lag must be catching up with him, and I say, "Why don't you go back to the hotel and put your feet up?"

"What are you going to do?" he asks, an edge to his voice.

I want to keep going, though I know he'd like me to return to the hotel with him. But I'm wound up, don't want to lie down, and I say, "I think I'll go to Shakespeare and Company, look through the books. Let's meet at that little café next to it in a few hours." He reluctantly agrees.

Inside Shakespeare and Company, George Whitman, the bookstore's famous owner, sits at his cash register, eating split pea soup out of a blue enamel pan. George reminds me of my father just before he died—bone thin, long face, gray hair, a little stooped over. He has that Yankee farmer look, a little sad, a little rundown. I'm looking through a copy of Stephen Spender's journals when a young American comes downstairs and says, "George, are you a praying man? Are you, George?" His tone is threatening. George begins pacing. The young man's voice rises, and George tries to escape by moving outside. The American keeps after him. "You'd better pray, George, you'd better pray that I don't become a famous writer and write about what a bullying old man you are."

My heart is pounding as I put down the book and follow them outside, looking around for someone to intercede. George is like a penned deer, jumping from one corner to another. The young man shoves George, then George makes a break for it back into the bookstore. I follow. The American suddenly stops and takes off. I'm trembling, wondering why I'm running into all this hostility. Inside, I ask George if he's OK. He nods, but he's clearly upset. I talk with him a bit and buy a copy of *The Fireside Readings*, which he signs.

I leave feeling sick and go to the café where I'll rendezvous with Dan. I sit down at an outside table. Two French women sit in front of me with their miniature greyhounds, feeding them scraps from the table, calling the dogs "Chérie" and "Princesse." The waiter is attending to them with an exasperated *"Oui, mesdames."* I'm thinking he'll be snotty with me, too, and I can't bear it, but before I can leave, he greets me. I struggle to smile, and he must have a sixth sense because he says, *"Ah, madame,"* in such a kind way that I sit back down and order tea. He nods, smiles, and says, *"Tout de suite."* I take out my journal to write, but find that I can't.

Writing about myself has been difficult. When I was in high school, I tried so hard to be everything my parents wanted me to be—I was an honor student, a yearbook editor, a class officer. I knocked myself out trying to make them happy. Most of my friends were boys—given my father's wrath, it was simply easier not to have boyfriends. He always told me, "It's not you I don't trust. It's the boys." I didn't believe him. In tenth grade, I found out he had been reading my diary since I was thirteen.

When the waiter brings my tea, he remains standing next to my table, looking toward the sidewalk. A man is staring straight at me, trying to get my attention; then he heads in my direction. But the waiter intercepts him, says something I can't hear, and the man retreats. The waiter turns and says, *"Pardon, madame,"* as if apologizing for the man. I say, *"Merci beaucoup, monsieur."* He bows and walks into the café. I'm trying not to cry. This man is protecting me, and for the first time I feel like part of the city, not a tourist. I write in my journal the name "Allan La Tour," and something breaks open.

It was the summer after my junior year. I had mustered the courage to ask my father, "What if I get asked out on a date?" My father said, "As long as you ask us a week in advance, and you go on a double date. And you have to be home by eleven."

When I was finally asked out, it was by an older boy, Allan La Tour. I asked permission a week in advance. Then on Saturday, the morning of my date, I was told I had to baby-sit for neighbors. "We promised the neighbors," my mother said. "We can't break our promise."

I shut myself in my room, playing Françoise loud enough to cover the sounds of my parents getting ready to go out themselves that evening. I couldn't win, not even by following the rules. I wanted freedom.

I snuck out that night, leaving my brother to baby-sit while my parents attended an American Legion Testimonial. At eleven o'clock, I walked through the front door. My parents had been called by the neighbors in the middle of their dinner and were waiting for me. My mother was crying, my brother was screaming that it wasn't his fault that the neighbors had come home early. My father took a belt to me—for the first and last time.

The waiter brings me fresh tea, and I pretend to write in order to hide my tear-filled eyes. By the end of June that year, Bobby Kennedy was dead, and de Gaulle's police had carried out a bloody crackdown on the student demonstrators and union workers. France was back under the thumb of de Gaulle, the one Frenchman my father admired. I was too tired to keep fighting and, as the news attested, people who fought for freedom or change were either arrested or shot anyway.

In my senior year of high school, I continued to wear pastel sweater sets when what I really wanted to wear was a black leather jacket and skintight pants like Françoise. That fall at the university, I was flunking my courses, my heart closed off to the joy of learning. I just didn't care anymore.

My only lifeline was an art course, and I chose to work on a life-size nude in pastels. But when someone stabbed holes through the breasts and pubic area, I gave up. I left the University of New Hampshire, telling no one, and moved in with a Vietnam vet who defied authority in every area of his life. When my parents discovered I was living "in sin," my father said, "Never come home, ever again." When I discovered I was pregnant, my mother begged him to let her take part in the wedding. I asked my father to give me away. He said, "Gladly." Three months before my son was born, my father killed himself.

I put my journal away, place twenty francs under my saucer, and leave. I don't know where I'm going, and I don't care. I pump my legs as fast as I can. I have dragged my father's dead body with me again, just as I dragged it to Oregon when my first husband's restlessness landed us there.

A legless man is lying on the sidewalk up ahead of me, and people are passing him as if he's not there. I slow down. He has a piece of rug under his head, a bottle tucked under his arm. I pass him, pick up speed, almost begin to run. After my father's death, the doctor told us he had been very ill with rheumatoid arthritis. My mother told me he was first struck down in Paris and spent a year in an Army hospital in Texas. I didn't understand how painfully ill he had been until we cleaned out his drawer and discovered he'd been living on Valium and twelve other medications. I was fighting for my freedom; he was fighting for his life.

I'm winded as I push through a crowd, find a bench, and sit down, hugging my backpack to my chest. It was never my dream to live in the isolated rural woods of Oregon with a husband and a three-year-old. The first time my husband came home drunk and beat me, I blamed myself. The second time, I blamed the war. When he came home drunk and destroyed one of my paintings, I understood I was fighting for my life. A year later we were divorced.

From my backpack I take out a bandanna, wipe my face, and look around. Students. They are bustling in all directions with their satchels and book bags. I take a deep breath and look behind me. I'm at the Sorbonne.

How ironic. I'd always wanted to be an artist, had planned on going to the Boston School of Fine Arts, and dreamed of attending the Sorbonne. But when I told this to my parents, my father said, "No. Art's a hobby. You'll study to be a teacher." Maybe it had been a hobby for him, when he painted landscapes in his youth and while hospitalized in Texas after the war, but it wasn't for me. "You'll get married, like everyone does," he said, "and you'll need something to fall back on if your husband dies."

Suddenly, I pop to my feet and look at my watch. Dan! I was supposed to meet him over half an hour ago. I rush back to the café, mad at myself for being derailed by my past, but he's not there. I race to our hotel. Dan doesn't deserve this. He's the only man who has ever gained my trust. We lived together for twelve years before he proposed marriage, and even then I was afraid of falling into an emotional lock step like the years in New Hampshire, when the world was defined by men and my feelings and desires didn't count. On his knee at a candlelit restaurant, he said, "All I want to do is make you happy, and I want you to quit your job so you can work on your novel." Then he added, "And someday, I'm taking you to Paris."

I reach the hotel. He's not in the lobby. I go to our room. He's not there either. I don't know what to do except stay in the room, hoping he comes back soon.

I pull out my journal and write: *All my life, I've been searching for something I can't identify, something missing in my life, something I long for, but eludes me like a word that floats just above the tongue, but won't land.*

I hear the key in the lock, and Dan comes into the room. His face is flushed. He's angry, or I think he's angry. "I'm so sorry. I got upset and left the café and—"

"What's the matter?" he says, as he sits down on the bed next to me and puts his arm around my waist. Now he looks perplexed and worried. "What happened?"

"You're not angry with me?" I say.

"No. Why should I be?" he says. "I figured I got the wrong café, so I came back here."

I throw my arms around him and cry. After I calm down, I finally tell him everything I've been going through. He says, "You'll figure it out before you leave. Just let it happen."

Over the next few days, we walk along the Seine, stop at the *bouquinistes*, kiss at the top of the Eiffel Tower. I discover that the pharmacies with their brightly lit green crosses are filled with diet aids, Parisian women are as elegant as legend has it, and the city's aesthetics extend even to the butchers, who decorate their cuts of meat with flowers. I love the abundance of flower boxes on the historic buildings, the smell and taste of yeasty baguette sandwiches with *jambon* followed by dark Italian coffee, the flirtatiousness of the French men. When a flatbed truck with striking Metro workers passes by, we yell *"Liberté! Egalité!"* and throw them the victory sign. But I am waiting for the proverbial other shoe to drop. I am waiting to make sense of this visit.

We save the Louvre for my birthday, and we discover that the *Mona Lisa* is quite small. But it's the painters and "hobbyists" who set up their easels and copy the masters' paintings that captivate me. Late afternoon, we stroll arm in arm along the Seine, and I stop to sit on a bench along the quay to watch an artist paint a landscape while I think about my practical father, who could approach art only as a hobby.

As I sit absorbing the experience, another memory returns.

Ten years after my father died, I returned home to help my mother clean out the basement. As I worked my way through the boxes, I found a few of my father's books—an Agatha Christie, a Hemingway, a Fitzgerald. I also found old boxes of pastels, books on how to draw the figure, and a 1940s correspondence course in cartooning and drawing. I noticed a wooden easel, covered in cloth, dusty, something I had often seen but never really looked at. When I pulled it out and threw back the cloth, I found a half-finished pastel of a hunter and his dog in the woods. The background was finished, as was the dog, but the hunter remained a penciled outline, like the ghost of a person unrealized.

I sit in stunned silence, wondering how I never put any of this together before. As I refocus on the artist, he wipes his brush on a rag, looks up, and smiles at me. I smile back and turn to the river. The Seine sparkles. I pivot slowly, and the panorama of the city seems all-embracing. I cover my mouth. The moment is strangely painful and liberating. When I glance over at Dan, he says, "What?"

I tell him about the memory, how sad I feel, not for myself, but for my father. Then I admit it—I *am* sad for me, sad that my father and I didn't have more time together, couldn't talk about art and creativity, the one thing we had in common. Dan takes my hand, and we walk to Notre Dame, where I light a candle for my father and finally let him go.

That night, as Dan showers and I wait to pack the toiletries, I'm singing another Françoise song when I look out the window and become too choked up to sing. The stars are out above the city and all is as quiet as this city can be at night. I release a long sigh, then take up Françoise's song again. She has been my muse throughout the years, and I thank her for lighting a path beneath my feet during the blackouts of my life, leading me to this city, to Paris, a place I can now call the city of my liberation.

My Humbling Chateau

Kate Adamek

"Something there is that doesn't love a wall," wrote the poet Robert Frost. I might have agreed before I, at the age of fifty-three, went off to build a wall myself. Listening to a spot about cheap ways to visit France on National Public Radio's "Savvy Traveler" program, I caught the words "live in a medieval village in France" and overlooked "help to reconstruct a ruined castle." But four months later, the grubby reality intruding on the gauzy romantic dream, I was building walls on the ramparts of le Castellas, a twelfth-century ruin of a castle high above the village of St. Victor la Coste in south-central France.

Lodged with the other participants in stone houses in the restored part of this Provençal village, I watched the Mediterranean sun honey-coat the autumn days and illuminate the soft surround of maritime Alps. Fairy-tale forests bordered the undulating carpet of vineyards and, to no one's greater amazement than my own, it turned out that I loved building walls. Loved it so much, I would return for three tours of duty over the next two years.

My master teachers were Henri and Simone Gignoux, along with their cast of young French artisans. Thirty-some years ago, the couple had unearthed from a wreck of rock on a hill the medieval part of St. Victor la Coste and the chateau hovering over it. In the modern era, St. Victor had become one of the pretty but ordinary villages that are scattered among the more renowned beauties of Gard. Firmly rooted on the vineyard-covered plain, St. Victor ignored the rubble of its past in favor of the present, which meant wine producing, Sunday *pétanque*, and pastis in the bar.

But Simone Gignoux, with a multigenerational history here, had infected her "foreigner" husband, Henri (who is from the French Alps, some sixty miles away), with her passion for the place. With wills no less formidable than the task ahead or the rocks themselves, husband and wife connived grants and contracts out of everyone, from the government of France to vintners' cooperatives—and the commune of St. Victor itself—and began their lifelong labor of love: using aged stones to renew old structures. They recruited young volunteer muscle to help with the masonry, stonecutting, tiling, paving, and dry stone walling. They called their enterprise La Sabranenque after the medieval family that had built the castle on the highest hill they owned.

It was during our orientation tour that I began to understand the classic Frenchness of the project. As my fellow volunteers (almost all

Americans) and I looked on, one of the French crew dribbled water slowly over a block of rust-red rock while another eased a hacksaw back and forth through its bulk. This use of methods devised somewhere around the birth of dirt puzzled us, a puzzlement strengthened daily as we worked with trowels and shovels and chisels—twins of those in an exhibit of Roman artifacts at the Palais des Papes in nearby Avignon. Was the organization really so strapped for cash that it couldn't afford power tools, or at least spades and rakes of lightweight metal alloys instead of the clunky wood and iron ones we lugged uphill every morning? How many daily scrubbings-out would the antediluvian black rubber buckets suffer before new galvanized aluminum ones took their place? The answers lie in one of those contradictions of character that make the French so confounding to Americans: In a country where the doggie bag is unheard-of and recycling is restricted to eco-fanatics, the frugal *femme d'intérieur* (housewife) is as standard as the bereted boulevardier. This "waste not, want not" code is carried out in every phase of life at La Sab, from today's tomato *farcis* transformed into tomorrow's pasta sauce to our living space: the medieval village of St. Victor revived in simple, tile-floored, thick-walled dwellings, with only the addition of running water and electricity and the absence of livestock stabled underneath to fix them in the present.

Equally Gallic is the adulation of ancient edifices to the point that an annual holiday is devoted to them. My first day at La Sab happened to coincide with this *"Jour du Patrimoine,"* when monuments, chateaux, and museums all over the country are free to the public, or in some cases open solely on this day. The gaggles of chic high-heeled women tottering up the rocky path to le Castellas that Sunday were an embodiment of the equal and contrary French obsessions with age-old tradition and the *dernière mode* (latest fashion). These passions are at the heart of La Sabranenque. For, as I came to learn, Henri and Simone are not interested in the exact re-creation of what once was. Their vision is of fresh creations that suggest the past while serving modern purposes—village picnics, vintners' wine parties, housing for volunteers.

To envision the enormity of the task Henri and Simone have undertaken, one has only to make the climb up to le Castellas, which was built by the Comte de Sabran to show who was who in the days before *Liberté, Egalité, Fraternité*. At the end of the ascent is instant time warp. A great curve of wall rises up, its narrow arrow slits frowning down on the unbidden. In the blink of an eye, one is a knight who has traveled long from far away, or Guinevere arriving at Camelot. Inside the castle's stone skeleton, sandstone and limestone walls reach up into broken towers, hug the rugged hillside, and suggest, like an architect's blueprint, a kitchen here, a great hall there, a chapel in the corner. The stones, which at a distance appear to be of a uniform sand hue, ripple up close with Rhone-water copper, the violet of new grapes, roof-tile terra cotta, the pale tones of high summer's lavender fields, olive-leaf green, and the grays of doves and donkeys.

It is exactly that sense of being both in the "now" and the "then" that I love most about rebuilding the ancient walls: the shifting of old stones back into structures designed before our Puritan predecessors were even a twinkle in Cromwell's eye; or three hundred years before Cromwell himself, a single Tudor monarch, and most of the kings of France were a sparkle in anyone's eye. Here and now, long after the bones of those busy men turned to dust, the stones remain. A thousand years ago, someone who lived, loved, and tasted the same kind of cheeses that I ate at Simone's dinner table each night had worked these stones. Each time I touched their raw surfaces, I sensed under my own hands those of someone who had worked the stones before me, a millennium ago.

I was sure he could not have looked much different than my first boss at La Sab, Pascal Parres.

Pascal and I stood eyeball to eyeball, but that was where the similarities ended. He was half my width, less than half my age, wiry, dreadlocked, and peppery. Wearing a face born of sturdy and stubborn genes—high-cheeked, long-nosed, black-eyed, and almond-hued with a sharp slash of mouth—he could have been painted by Holbein, and in his very French face I imagined I could see the original builders of le Castellas. Pascal had found his way to La Sabranenque by electing to do twenty months of alternative service instead of ten months of military. Trained in stonework, Pascal was an ardent stonemason with a fleck of flinty perfectionism that could at times go to war with his creativity. It was Pascal who taught me respect for the stones, to look at them as living beings. "Stones are your friends," he would say gravely. "You must love the stones. Each one is beautiful in her own way. Each one belongs somewhere exactly right for her and for the wall."

As with all passions, there were times when love teetered on loathing. *"Putain!"*—Whore!—he would swear when the chosen stone refused to meet the moment's need. The stones could be a fickle lot, lying there enticing as sirens, calling, "I am the one, come to me!"—only to be found exactly *not* the one after a back-wrenching struggle to lift it onto fast-drying mortar. Henri, the master of us all, frowned on maltreatment of the stones, but there were moments when only hefting a stone vigorously onto the discard pile would satisfy frustrated passion. The pile was, after all, only temporary—one person's discard being another's treasure.

In spite of his notoriously short fuse, Pascal stretched the limits of his patience. Time and again he explained to me the vertical and two horizontal lines of walls with which one must align; the proper placement of stones; the optimal thickness and wetness of mortar and how to spread it just so with the edge of the trowel (*"Putain!* Never, ne-ver on the flat!"*); and how small, thin stones set vertically down in the gaps between big ones served as reinforcement.

Learning to see the right stone was the most important skill of this craft. You had to learn to spot it in the heaps of fallen-down castle that lay everywhere around us. Never, *ne-ver* give it a trial run by placing it on top of another unmortared stone. This was one of Henri's mortal sins of masonry, and God help you if he should catch you *en flagrante.*

Henri was clearly born for the stage: Not only was he blessed with an impressive Cyrano de Bergerac nose and all-seeing ice-blue eyes that could slice with a glance, but he possessed a voice with the heft of the Pont du Gard. Only his obvious yearning to teach, to have me understand deep in my heart, eyes, and hands the beauty of this ancient skill, kept me from being flattened by his noisy, arm-flailing critiques.

"*Regardez le ciel!*" (Look at the sky!) he would cry to the heavens. "*Respirez!*" (Breathe!) He delivered his sermon on the mount, hailing first the great glories of nature and her works all around us, and then the miraculous capacity of stones—correctly laid down, of course— to outlast kings and kingdoms, gods and monsters, and all the sufferings and joys of this mortal coil. In this art and craft, we mortals have the chance to achieve an immortality largely unknown in modern life: to leave a space ordered and whole again where rubble had previously reigned. And not to do one smidgen of harm to our lovely earth as we do so.

It was not all fun and the beauty of stones, however, this volunteering on the rock pile. Each day began too early, with the usual nonbreakfast of the French: coffee and yesterday's bread to dunk in it, followed too soon by the worst part of the day, the hated climb up the hill. I began to take pride in my notoriety as the last one up, defying any of the young chits with defined calf muscles to go as slowly as I. I felt reinforced in my tardiness when I learned that the prize for getting up the hill first was making mortar—a back-breaking task of mixing sand, concrete, and water into just the right consistency while circling the pile with the devil's own speed. A couple of times I arrived in time for the job of water-sprinkler, flinging handfuls of water from a bucket ("Not so much!" "Too much, too much!

Do you want to make a lake here?") while dodging the flying shovel blades and hard young bodies of the mad mortar merry-go-round. I quickly learned to adjust my arrival time.

The French seem to have something against bucket brigades, another difference between the French and Americans—and a frequent cause of grumbling. Some days, all we did was shift stones from one difficult-to-reach place up to another along slim tracks edged by long downhill drops. But the French were the bosses, so we dutifully transported armloads of rock for hours on end, dreaming of lunch and wondering why the hell we were here when we could have done this kind of *merde* in our own backyards.

But the possibility of uncovering something really old was not to be had in our own backyards. One day at a chateau called Gicon, about a twenty-minute drive from St. Victor, I was assigned to work with Alain, an old La Sab hand. We dug through a hillside of ground cover, roots, stones, and dirt to locate the foundation of the original outer wall, built by the Romans. Coated in layers of sweat and ambient dust and dirt, I was in a repetitive-motion trance when I realized that the rock I had just picked up had a shape no rock was ever born with. I held up the loam-encrusted, powdery terra-cotta piece and showed it to Alain.

"*Mais c'est intéressant!*" Alain pronounced, taking the two-by-three-inch curve of pottery in his hand. He told me it was the handle from a Roman jug, maybe third or second century, and handed it back. Holding an artifact so old that most of my ancestors had not yet reached their launching pads for America when it was created, I was struck with wonder and delight at the stubborn durability of the human race. And I felt suddenly graced by the dust of its ages settling upon me.

Alexander Pope famously wrote, "A little learning is a dangerous thing." By my third tour of duty at le Castellas, I knew just enough to be dangerous to myself. With regard to wall-building, I believed, I'd been there, done that. I had all the T-shirts. I was feeling especially smug about the topping of walls because once, in my earliest La Sab days, Henri had taken one look at my first attempt at a wall top and with a flick of the trowel scraped the whole thing to the ground as he belted out the three absolutes of wall tops: strong, durable, and deeply set. My lesson learned, I took minutes on end to set each stone strongly and deeply—to be unmovable by nature or man.

Then, one day, three of us were rebuilding a small wall just off the old kitchen area inside le Castellas: Rachel, a young Englishwoman with excellent French and several weeks' experience at La Sab; Wanda, a fresh and eager new recruit; and veteran me. We had been left to do our work unsupervised, which was unusual for volunteers. Each time Henri stopped on his inspection rounds to eye our progress, we held our breaths until he nodded a grudging approval. Adding to our apprentice angst was the nature of our assignment. For rather than starting a wall from scratch, we had the far more difficult job of patching and rebuilding on the foundations of an existing one, which is something like putting together a puzzle with a number of missing original pieces for which we had to find workable replacements.

The worst of it seemed to be behind us, with only the wrap-up task of topping the wall left, when Henri came out of nowhere throwing verbal punches. And not at Rachel and Wanda, with their slapdash, slop-top style—at me, the good girl, doing it exactly as he had told me to two years before.

It was déjà vu as Henri, glaring at *my* wall, his huge nose red with fury, fired away: "You are taking too much time! The mortar is drying out before you get a stone anywhere near it!" And, "Does this total *merde* you are doing suggest a ruin?! *Non! PAS DU TOUT!*"

Between my perilous little learning and a mild case of attention deficit disorder, I had missed the fact that two years ago, we had been working on an outside wall, part of the fortifications of le Castellas. This was an *inside* wall, which would never be required to keep out the barbarian hordes.

"How long have you been coming here now—don't you know anything yet?! If I want an outside wall, I will put it outside! When I say I want it to look like a ruin that is what I want!" With that, he took his trowel and pried up and off, casting into oblivion every single one of my carefully set stones before delivering a final blow: "Now you are looking at me like my donkey looks. Stop looking like a donkey and just do the work!" (There are those who either didn't remember or don't believe he said this last part, which was over the top even for Henri—but I heard it clearly with my own two donkey ears.)

What was left in the ashes of my formerly confident self sizzled with indignation. *How dare he, when I was doing exactly as he . . . and in front of everybody! Who does he think he is? I GIVE UP!*

Later I learned from eyewitnesses that none of them had thought of the proceedings as anything but ordinary (except for the alleged donkey remark). They had all come under this kind of fire with the regularity of the sunrise. Later, too, I learned from a long-time expat a peculiar tenet of French culture: Those whom the French love, they criticize.

But at that moment, exactly as I had as a Catholic-school girl scolded by Sister Mary Ambrose, I wanted only to become invisible. Failing that, I slunk away, knowing as sure as *Dieu* made little green *pommes* that I was going to cry. Carrying myself as though I were made of crystal, I hid behind a big screen of brambly bush against the chapel wall.

Twenty minutes of stifled weeping and gnashing of teeth later, I was together enough to come out, if not to go back to work. I decided to take my trowel and go home. A pleasant Swiss gentleman sitting on the wall just outside the door of le Castellas saved me from myself. Visiting the area with his family, he stopped me to ask about our activities up here. I morphed instantly into Friendly American mode, and found myself explaining our work, *my work*, to preserve a small bit of the French patrimony. I talked of the section of outer wall I'd built my first year, the pavement I'd laid last week, the kitchen I'd bailed buckets of rubble from the other day. By the time I was introduced to his wife and polite, blond daughters, my fifty-five-year-old self was back in charge, ready to return to the work that had brought me back year after year to La Sabranenque.

Keeping a healthy distance between myself and the ill-omened wall, I looked for somewhere else to screw up. Pascal was busy building a dry wall with two young Bulgarian women. He didn't really need more assistants, but he let me join them anyway. I knew he was being kind, probably because he himself had often tasted Henri's displeasure. And he must have understood that I was in a delicate state, for during the rest of my morning's efforts, not once did the word *"putain"* come from Pascal's mouth in regard to my work—a first.

By the end of the weekend, I could be within five feet of Henri without flashbacks. In my remaining weeks, I never heard a discouraging word from him. In fact, he frequently picked me to work with him (generally considered an honor), assigned me to supervise new volunteers on simple projects, actually praised my work a number of times, and once, in my last week, gave me a solo on the exact kind of wall reconstruction that had been my fall from grace. Only this one was even tougher, because it was in a tight corner and more difficult to get at, its top much higher and harder to see and lay down.

All the butterflies of Gard inhabited my stomach as I awaited Henri's appraisal of the finished product. He studied my work with his microscopic vision, reaching out to tweak a rock here, test a rock there. Then, backing away, he nodded and said, loud and clear and in front of everyone, *"C'est parfait!* That was a very difficult piece of work and you have done it perfectly—better maybe than even I could have." He patted me on the shoulder with his big, dusty workman's paw. I grew as tall as the Eiffel Tower, as grand with victory as the Arc de Triomphe. Henri has approved! Who in the world would want to be anyone but me?

Never in my life in the States have I experienced the acid sweetness that I encountered in France. Nowhere else on earth have I translated criticism as regard, have I prized praise as highly as a rare vintage wine. In no other place have I been so bloodied and bruised, physically and emotionally, and savored it so much. Maybe all this captivating contrariness is located equally in other cultures and climes. But for me it is rooted firmly in France, about ten miles northwest of Avignon, in an unremarkable little village called St. Victor la Coste. And I will always go back for more.

Paris Lip
Ayun Halliday

My mother served as the *Indianapolis Star's* fashion editor in her early twenties, when attractive professional women modeled themselves on Jackie Kennedy. I have a photograph of her and several other fashion editors flanking Charlton Heston, costumed as the hunky young Moses on the set of *The Ten Commandments*. Clearly, she was going places. Then she gave it all up to have me.

In that Moses picture, she looks as if she's hiding a watermelon under her pretty spring suit. When I was in high school, my mother resumed her job, covering the semiannual collections in New York for a readership whose tastes ran to bright golf sweaters appliquéd with funny animals. In the fall of 1990, the *Star* sent her to Paris, her first trip abroad. I went along as a sort of inept translator, my schoolgirl vocabulary in ruins despite two previous visits. Mom arrived in

Paris with the short hair, bright lipstick, and distinctive spectacle frames of the fashion pen's reigning queen bees. But whereas they knifed their way through the crowd in expensive, body-skimming shades of charcoal, battleship, and ink, her uniform ran toward pale denim shirtfronts tucked into darker denim ranch skirts that rode high over the abdomen. Further distancing herself from the Cruella de Vil crowd in the City of Light, she'd taken to wearing Birkenstock sandals with socks, a crime against *la mode* that she'd picked up from her daughter.

I operated, then as now, twenty thousand leagues below the radar of the glamour editors. My anachronistic, anti-ironing-board, kitchen-sink romanticism was perfectly suited to my Salvation Army budget. Alas, the thrift store plunder bursting from my closet never congealed into an identifiable style. I was a little bit country, a little bit rock 'n' roll, slightly ratty, rarely flattered, ever stained, mostly Shakespearean by way of Woodstock.

I packed my bag with an eye toward cutting a dashing figure.

Our digs in the Duminy Vendome, an old hotel off the rue de Rivoli, were fairly plush; the food was plentiful; and I was wildly in love, flush with an infatuation as delicious and short-lived as the lone bead of nectar squeezed from a honeysuckle blossom. Unfortunately for my mother, she, not my lover, was my traveling companion. Mom had envisioned a fun mother-daughter escapade: We would arrive a week before Fashion Week, rent a car, and tour Normandy and the Loire Valley. At Giverny, we would picnic within spitting distance of Monet's infernal water lilies. After glutting ourselves on the picturesque, we would roll back into Paris, where Mom would cover the collections.

My poor mother. All I wanted to do was close my eyes and wake up in the cramped candlelit bedroom of my new boyfriend. If Satan had materialized on the wrought iron balcony, I would have swapped my mother and my soul for Wylie in a nanosecond. Mom knew it, but tried not to show it. Just before we rendezvoused with our rental car, we were loading butter and marmalade onto uninspired croissants in our hotel's basement breakfast room when a young couple sat down at the next table. The man was tall and Asian, with a long ponytail hanging down his back. He looked just like Wylie. I thought I would swoon. If only I could lay my palm on his back and feel his heartbeat through the thin cotton of his shirt. That was all I wanted, just a crumb to tide me over for the next twelve days.

"I'll bet you miss Wylie," Mom ventured uncertainly. Only 288 hours to go, I thought, not counting the return flight. I grunted an affirmative to my mother as I nonchalantly shook a Gauloise out of my pack. If I couldn't be with my lover, at least I could pretend to be French.

Under cover of jet lag, I caught up on the sleep I had missed since taking up with Wylie six weeks earlier. I was a real dud in the company department. Mealtimes were the hardest. In the car, I could sleep. Tourist attractions offered partial distraction from my Wylie-less state with their informational plaques, often helpfully translated into English. I learned quite a bit about the landing at

Omaha Beach, the Bayeux tapestry, Monet's love of Japanese wood-cuts, and the monk-designed formal vegetable garden at the chateau at Villandry. Sometimes I got pissy, like when Mom whispered to me to watch my bag as we passed through a street market en route to the famous cathedral in Chartres. When one is suffering from the pangs of lovesickness, the pragmatic comments of a mother do not go unpunished.

Back at our Right Bank hotel, we found our mailbox overflowing with invitations to the designers' shows. Mom raked through the pile, plucking out envelopes from the real players. Not every journalist who ventures to Paris makes the cut for the hottest shows' guest lists, so every big name came as a relief. "Oh, good, here's Ralphie," she said, pushing her red glasses higher on the bridge of her nose. (To the best of my knowledge, Ralphie and my mother's personal relationship does not extend beyond the labels in her denim shirtwaists and the approving opinions expressed in the *Indianapolis Star.*)

"Oh, here's one at the Ritz," she said, picking up a large square card edged in lipstick pink. "The Paris Lip? I have no idea who that is. Oh, look, it says Lauren Bacall is going to make a presentation."

That night, in the wee hours, we woke to the unmistakable sound of enthusiastic copulation. The acoustics of the air shaft were such that our neighbors' every gasp and groan reverberated with complete clarity. We lay rigid in our beds, my mother and I, unable to ignore what was happening so close at hand. Wishing with all my might that the lovers would achieve a speedy, muffled climax, I couldn't help observing that at least someone was getting her money's worth out of a Paris hotel room. She vocalized without inhibition, as people do when their mothers aren't within earshot.

"Sounds like a chicken," Mom observed grimly, staring at the ceiling.

I am indebted to the Paris Lip for giving me a gander at two glamorous old legends, the Ritz and Bacall. As we entered the famed hotel, a worried-looking public relations woman seized Mom's elbow. "I'm so glad you're here," she said in an accent much like my own. Mom smiled politely and introduced her to me. The woman beamed. "We're so glad you could make it, too! Are you having fun?" I accepted the press materials she offered with an unimpressed nod, making it clear that I wasn't some little girl with braces accompanying Mommy to work. My mother seemed pleased with my journalistic sangfroid.

We entered a conference room worthy of Louis XIV. The enormous oil paintings hanging between elegantly draped windows were as diverting as any in the Louvre, but without the tourist hordes shoving to get close enough to be disappointed by the dark little *Mona Lisa*. Ten thousand dollars' worth of cut flowers towered on antique tables. The chairs that had been arranged in rows before the small stage were of the polished-wood, nonfolding variety. The room was, in a word, ritzy.

We took our seats and, at the appointed hour, the heavy inlaid doors were pulled shut, the lights dimmed, and Prince's "Kiss" issued at thunderous volume from giant speakers flanking a large screen. Gripped by a Pavlovian response to the combination of darkness and music, the room erupted in applause at the first projected slide, a giant profile of a shocking-pink mouth with the Paris Lip logo scrawled above it, as if on a bathroom mirror. A triumphant cascade of images followed, flashed in time to Prince's beat. Scowling models with flawless skin flaunted fire-engine-red lips as thick as caterpillars. A feline teen in a fishnet muscle T arranged his queen-size maw in a coy expression. Disembodied mouths bit strawberries, suckled striped drinking straws, and licked gloss from their freakishly large lips with photogenic tongues.

Like Scarlett O'Hara pinching her cheeks before the ball, I started gnawing my bottom lip in readiness for the moment when the lights would come back up. Sidelong glances revealed that I wasn't the only one chewing my way toward the onscreen ideal. None of us had made much headway before Lauren Bacall stepped into a single dramatic beam illuminating an old-money podium alongside the screen. That was a thrill.

Generally, fashion shows attract freshly minted celebrities of questionable staying power who sit ringside wearing sunglasses and platinum necklaces with their first names spelled in diamond-studded script. Ms. Bacall, the girl who had asked Humphrey Bogart if he knew how to whistle, was the genuine article, still classy and compelling in an unstructured silk suit. She paused graciously while her audience applauded in joyous recognition. Assuming a pair of half-glasses—for the record, they made her look smart, not old—she began reading from prepared notes. "Cindy Crawford embodies the beauty of full, sensuous lips," she observed, as the supermodel's giant mug loomed onscreen. Bacall ignored Cindy's other celebrated attributes, such as her unlikely combination of weight and height, her boys' department hips, and the big brown mole that she would have had surgically removed if she were Doris in Accounts Payable.

More famous lovelies followed, all of whom passed Ms. Bacall's labial muster. A lusty scream arose at a slide of Mick Jagger at the height of his powers, thirty years earlier. Even Lauren Bacall—Betty, I believe she is called by her friends—catcalled at the sinewy lad leering in black and white.

"Mick! Now there's a set of lips!" The slide carousel advanced, giving us a '70s-era portrait of Mick and his then-wife Bianca with their unsurprisingly large-mouthed daughter, Jade. "Bianca had great lips, too," Bacall cooed. "And just look at little Jade! Why, we could call them the First Family of Lips . . . except they're not a family anymore."

The quip went over like canned tuna at a Greenpeace gathering. Glances were exchanged, and there was even a bit of faint French-inflected hissing. Ms. Bacall, ever the trooper, hustled on to her next line. I wondered why she was so hard up that she would sign on as mouthpiece for this tawdry outfit. Squinting toward the podium, I saw that her mouth was no larger than my own. Shouldn't the Paris Lip suits have insisted on a spokeswoman who exemplified the standard of beauty they were trying to establish—someone like, oh, I don't know, Bianca Jagger?

Finally, Bacall fulfilled her contract and stalked offstage to a smattering of polite applause. An American employee of the Paris Lip took the podium, gushing about how it felt to "share" the stage with the timeless beauty who had preceded her. She talked at length about the exciting developments in the field of cosmetic science that had led to her company's remarkable new procedure, in which skimpy lips are plumped up through a series of nearly painless shots administered in the offices of trained physicians.

"No more faking it with a liner pencil," she trumpeted in an approximation of you-tell-it-girlfriend frankness, before intimating that we were in for a special treat. Dr. Diderot Bœuftoit, one of the Paris Lip's foremost practitioners, was on hand to perform a live demonstration. The French journalist ahead of us blanched. "Ooh, I can't watch," Mom whimpered in the queasy whine she reserves for impending cinematic violence.

The doctor bounded onstage, gathered the speaker in his arms, and kissed her on both cheeks as she giggled. He looked like he'd have been more at home in a gold lamé G-string on the beaches of Biarritz. He had brown feathered hair, a Roman nose, and the adorable grin of a highly successful rake. A gold chain glinted in the tangle of chest hair manfully asserting itself at his open collar. He was the only medical professional I've ever seen who managed to make a lab coat look slinky.

"Can we bring out Christine," the Lip rep called. A scrawny figure emerged from a door behind the stage, took a few tentative steps on spiked metallic heels, and stopped. She had the trembling air of an aging doe trying to pass as a fawn in skintight studded denim. The rigors of maintaining her emaciated figure and deep nutmeg tan had left her haggard. Large, dark eyes peered out from under a dry mane of unnatural ash blonde. And her lips! Great bacon rinds liberally frosted in bubblegum pink and outlined with pencil several shades darker.

Fortunately, harsh judgment, unlike extreme heat, does not produce visible effects. If it did, poor Christine would have withered under our toxic gaze. Gallantly, Dr. Bœuftoit rescued this lonely creature from our critical high beams, leading her tenderly to a sort of medical lounge chair that had been rolled out from behind the screen. A nurse joined them, bearing a tray of syringes and cotton balls. A technician trained a video camera on Christine's face, which then appeared, huge, on the screen. The nurse swabbed her lips with cotton balls until no trace of frosty pink remained. It couldn't have been pleasant for someone like Christine to have her giant, naked lips scrutinized by strangers.

"As you can see, Christine already has gorgeous, very sexy, full lips," the doctor purred through a wireless mike. "Zis is her sixth treatment. It is not necessary, she could stop now and remain happy, but after zis application, she will be even more beautiful, more sensuous." It struck me that Christine had a compulsion on par with anorexia, a self-assessment so distorted that it was now leading her to further inflate her already pneumatic lips.

The doctor explained how he would make a series of injections at the lip line. He drew some vertical stripes on Christine's mouth with grease pencil so he'd know where to place the surgical steel tip of his syringe. Selecting a gleaming instrument, he bent over his patient, blocking her body—though we still had an excellent view of her giant video head. Her nostrils flared and tears sprang into her eyes as the needle pierced her skin. Those of us who could bear to look writhed in sympathy, moaning. "Shh, shh, shh," Dr. Bœuftoit hissed, ostensibly to Christine. He seemed to be out of his element in a situation requiring something more than gigolo charm. He fumbled with the tray, sending some surgical steel tools clattering to the floor. "Ees OK! Ees OK," he reassured us before whispering urgently to the nurse in his native tongue.

Grabbing the needle, he reapplied himself to the task, plunging in another stripe of animal byproducts. Christine yipped. She probably would have screamed if the big syringe hadn't restricted her mouth's movement. The doctor hiccupped, reflexively trying to diffuse the tension with the remains of his formerly ingratiating laugh. "It is not so bad, is it, *chérie?*" he cajoled. The enormous head bravely indicated that it was not by rotating on its neck a fraction of a millimeter to either side. The doctor turned to face the press. "You see? I told you so," he accused playfully, shaking a hairy, jeweled finger in our direction. Beads of sweat on his skinny upper lip reflected the light from the elegant chandeliers. I glanced at the American representative. She clung to the podium, looking like she'd been shipwrecked. "OK, OK," the doctor muttered under his breath, psyching himself up for injection number three.

"She's bleeding!" someone in the crowd gasped. We buzzed impotently. If only there had been a representative of Amnesty International present. "OK, yes, sometimes zis happens," the doctor barked, his handsome face contracting into a harassed mask of such stereotypical French indignation that I longed for a baguette and a beret to complete the effect. "It is nothing, *oui?*" The speakers crackled and popped as his body mike malfunctioned mid-rant. The video camera operator left his tripod unmanned, dug under the doctor's lab coat, and grappled with the battery pack clipped to his belt.

The nurse applied pressure to Christine's wound with a strip of gauze. Christine's eyes, as big as manhole covers onscreen, darted frantically in what was now a silent horror movie. The technician was not able to wholly restore the doctor's mike. Once the nurse had stopped the bleeding, he completed the injections efficiently, but his narration issued forth as an alien language of gabble and squawks that frequently cut out altogether. Anyone who has ever taken part in a junior high school assembly would have recognized immediately that he had lost his audience for good. Contemptuous chatter sprang up like brushfires. I'm amazed he wasn't pelted with spitballs.

At long last he whipped off Christine's paper drape, helped her to her feet, and presented her to us as a "new" woman. She leaned weakly on his arm, hiding behind her long bangs, which had the unsettling effect of shielding everything but her much-abused lips. I understood then why we hadn't seen the Paris Lip inflicted on a higher-status model.

At the sparsely attended reception, I wolfed down dozens of canapés from trays passed by waiters in formal attire. Our monogrammed plates came equipped with sterling claws to hold our champagne flutes. I'd never seen anything so cunning. They justified the last hour far more than Lauren Bacall, who, rather than mingle, had decamped to her suite, presumably to wait for the check to clear. The publicist tacked toward us, apparently trying to make it look like she was weaving her way through a great crowd. "So?" she cried, with hollow gaiety. "Have you ever seen anything like it?"

"No," Mom replied, cramming another canapé into her mouth to escape elaboration. The publicist clung to us, having identified the *Indianapolis Star* as her client's last, best hope. I tried to imagine the women of my hometown driving their children to school, shopping at the Castleton Mall, and attending services at Second Prez with lips the size of those edible wax ones we used to chew around Halloween. At times I've adopted a hipper-than-thou stance toward my fellow Hoosiers, but this was not one of them. I'm happy to opine that no self-respecting female Indianapolite would pay someone to inject butcher's refuse into any part of her body, let alone her lips, even if it was to help raise funds for the Cub Scout Jamboree. That publicist was *merde* out of luck, as we used to say in Indiana, *pardonnez mon français.*

As we were leaving, I felt Mom's elbow in my ribs. I turned my head slowly, expecting Lauren Bacall—or at least Cindy Crawford. Instead I followed her gaze to the elevators, where Dr. Bœuftoit stood talking to the Paris Lip rep. Christine leaned against the wall behind them, gingerly fingering the outlying borders of her swollen gob. The rep had the air of a geeky high school overachiever, vacillating between dismay that the other kids had trashed her homecoming dance and elation that the coolest boy in school was teasing her about it in a nice way. The golden elevator doors opened with a suitably discreet and moneyed swoosh. The doctor slid his hand inside Christine's studded outfit via a peekaboo panel cut into the area between her shoulder blades. He steered her into the elevator, pressing a button to take them to the guest rooms on the upper floors. Mom nodded with the canary-swallowing expression of one who has not been fooled for a second. So he was a gigolo, and Christine the worn-out old showgirl who loved him! God, it was so French. I suddenly realized that I had not thought of Wylie once during my Paris Lip experience.

Later, I discovered that Mom had stuffed two pink linen cocktail napkins bearing the Ritz's logo into my purse while the public relations wretch was bending her ear. "I can't believe you stole these," I said as I folded them into my backpack for the return trip.

"Well," she shrugged, pulling on her Claude Monet sleeping shirt and getting into bed, "I wanted you to have something special to remember our trip to Paris." As if the Paris Lip press kit weren't souvenir enough.

The Source of the Seine

Georgia Hesse

Evelyn and I sat in the lobby bar of the Trianon Palace near Versailles's gardens and sipped wine with the manager. "And where will you go tomorrow?" he asked, with a distinct lack of interest. "Back to America?"

"*Non, monsieur,*" I replied. "We are going to find the source of the Seine." (In French, the word *source* usually refers to an underground spring; I used it for both its English and French meanings.)

"Ah, *oui,*" he muttered, absently. "*Les sources de la Seine.* Of course, we learned all about that in school, but I have never . . ." He broke off, suspicious as a lizard. "*Les sources,*" he muttered darkly. "*Pourquoi?*" But why? Were two wandering foreign women about to exploit a mother lode of undefined enormous wealth that by all rights should be reserved to the French?

About noon the next day, our car slid to a stop before the medieval ramparts of Provins. Only fifty-five miles from Paris, we had driven into the Middle Ages. Time to take a little something, at least a *kir*, with which to salute the shades of this walled town's past: Abélard and Héloïse, Edmund of Lancaster and the Red Rose. At the pretty café-hotel Aux Vieux Remparts, the waitress hummed to herself. "*Eh, bien. Deux kirs.* You are on vacation. To go where?"

"*Aux sources de la Seine, madame,*" we answered, in unison.

"Ah, *oui!* In school . . . I remember . . . they are . . . *pourquoi?*" We heard at least three question marks. She retreated and glanced at us sideways. The French mind mistrusts direct answers. It delights in intricacy and envies the ability to obfuscate. The French want outsiders to know a lot about *la belle France*—but are mortified when they actually do.

We cut southeast through the rich flatlands of Grande Champagne, moving at the pace of truffle-snuffling pigs. I lusted (no other word will do) after every hamlet, church, museum, forest, cozy café, and comforting inn along the river.

Two Champagnes compose the countryside familiar to American travelers, both lying east and slightly north of Paris. First comes to mind the region of Reims, of bottles and bubbly and Brie. In Hautvillers the blind seventeenth-century monk and cellar master Dom Pierre Pérignon created (or perhaps didn't) the first proper champagne, and cried out (or perhaps didn't) to his fellows, "Come quickly! I am tasting stars!" (It's a pretty story, so I choose to believe it.)

The second Champagne conjures up not laughter and frivolity but stillness and sorrow: The names on the land are Ardennes (Celtic for deep forest) and Argonne, Château-Thierry and the Marne—fading trumpet blasts from World Wars I and II.

Evelyn and I meandered southeast, Seine-side, in the third, least-known Champagne, where the soil is more clay than chalk. We shared a fascinating companion: Anthony Glyn—in book form. His *Seine* begins this way: "Like the Jordan, the Ganges, the Rhine, the Seine is a holy river." Glyn goes on to write that "from earliest times," a goddess named Sequana lived deep in a valley between wooded hills in Burgundy. Her cult was as great as the healing springs that seeped from the good earth, grew into the Seine, and ran away to Paris.

Our first night en route, we snugged into the Moulin du Landion near the edge of Dolancourt (pop. 145), a hop west of Bar-sur-Aube, where in 1814 the king of Prussia, the emperor of Austria, and the czar of Russia met in the local chateau to discuss what to do about France. That is the only thing that ever happened in Bar-sur-Aube.

From our flowery inn and its millrace, we visited three ghosts: Saint Bernard in Absinthe Valley, where that son of a nobleman founded Clairvaux Abbey, soul of the Cistercian order named after Cîteaux in Burgundy; General Charles de Gaulle, at his simple home in Colombey-les-Deux-Eglises, near the pompous Cross of Lorraine memorial; and Joan of Arc in Domrémy-la-Pucelle, where she first heard her saintly voices.

One day we idled in Troyes: Troyes where ladies wore wimples and knights wenched; Troyes of the medieval markets that gave the world the system of troy weights; Troyes of the *andouillettes* (tripe sausage) massacre.

That is a story too good to be skipped. Near the end of the sixteenth century, Troyes belonged to a political group called La Ligue, governed by an eleven-year-old boy, Claude de Guise, who was opposed to the French Royalists. When the raging Royalists moved into his city, Claude hid out in the cathedral while the invading troops took the Saint-Denis quarter, where *andouillettes* were made. Famished (so French), the Royalists fell upon the *andouillettes* (and perhaps some wine, as well?) and slipped into, as Michelin says, "complete euphoria." While sleeping it off, as it were, they were slaughtered by the city's defenders. Talk about food wars!

We had admired the sixteenth-century rose window of the Cathédrale St. Pierre and St. Paul and the flying buttresses of the Basilique St. Urbain; we approved the Rodin sculptures and fauvist paintings in the Musée d'Art Moderne. Lunch hour had arrived, sacred as ever in rural France. In the vast Bistroquet, I asked our waiter for a simple *sandwich mixte* (ham and cheese) to be made with the regional, tangy Maroilles cheese. "We have no *sandwich mixte*, alas," the waiter said. "I am desolated."

Hm. I remembered a wile of Anthony Glyn's. "May I have some thin slices of ham, *s'il vous plaît?*"

"*Mais oui, madame.*"

"And bread?"

"Certainly."

"And a glass of Burgundy? And perhaps some cheese?"

"Perhaps Maroilles, madame?"

The waiter winked. I made a delicious sandwich.

Next day, Madame of the Moulin helped us pack our car. She had been an admirable and solicitous *patronne*, even loaning us $20 worth of francs apiece when we checked in on a holiday weekend. (In France, banks frequently close on Friday noons, reopening smartly on Tuesday mornings.)

"*Les Américains*, they are always *en mouvement*," she pronounced—with some envy, I thought. "Where now?"

We did not look at each other. "*Les sources de la Seine*."

"In history . . . where are . . . *pourquoi?*"

Stately poplars, like golden wands, lined the Seine's grassy banks. "At least we're not just roaming," Evelyn said. "This trip is beginning to have a theme." We wiggled west to Bar-sur-Seine (near Chaource, named for a cheese) and entered Burgundy just north of Châtillon-sur-Seine.

Châtillon is a coquette of a town with an unsurpassed treasure: the great vase of Vix. The hammered bronze giant, five feet six inches high, weighs 459 pounds and can hold 1,100 liters—of wine, do you suppose? Who made it? How, where, and why? Only the when is known: during the sixth century B.C. (I like to think it was a Greek hot tub for Sequana redux.)

In Châtillon I encountered, not for the first time, the perversity of the French *petite-bourgeoise* who does not know, does not want to know, or does not want to admit that she does not know. It happened in a bookstore.

"*Bonjour, madame.* Have you a book on the history of the Seine?"

"*L'histoire?*"

"*Oui.*"

"Of what?"

"The Seine."

"What is the title?"

"I don't know; that's what I wish to know."

"And the author?"

"I don't know the author. That's why I'm asking you."

She smirked. She had triumphed. "How can I help you if you don't know what you want?"

The *patronne* of the Hôtel Côte d'Or inquired about our route as we checked out. Our response, as usual, "*Aux sources de la Seine, madame.*"

"There, there is nothing. I have the word of friends. Nothing. *Pourquoi?*"

We followed back roads to the abbey of Fontenay, as impressive and solid as it must have been in the twelfth century. We approached delicious Semur-en-Auxois along the rue de Paris. A bank of pastel houses climbed a pink granite cliff above the river Armançon. We made a noteworthy promenade here, atop the antique ramparts in the shade of lime trees, passing the eighteenth-century hospital-mansion where the town's governor once lived. His wife, though said to be priggish, was a sweetheart of Voltaire's. The French don't quit.

Gaiety turned to gloom as the afternoon wore on. We circled, and backed, turned and twisted—aimless. Neither map nor sign indicated we were anywhere near *les sources*. The sky darkened; a chilly wind swept up. Rain spat upon the windshield. We were getting close to trafficky Dijon.

Voilà! Surely a wide spot named St. Seine-l'Abbaye would shelter the holy source.

It proved the site only of a small church and a bar, out of which staggered an adult ragamuffin. "Ask where it is," I snapped, slowing the car. "If he says *pourquoi* I will run over him!"

"Where," shouted Evelyn, "are *les sources de la Seine?*"

"What? Who?" His head wobbled; his knees buckled. "Who knows? *Pourquoi? Pourquoi? Pourquoi?*"

I gunned away. Fat drops oozed from low clouds. Suddenly, there, there on the left—a small, poorly lettered sign: *"Les Sources."*

The narrow trail, winding and tedious, entered a lonely valley squeezed by foggy hills. Sad. Forbidding. I tried and failed to imagine the grand Roman temples, the sacred bathing pools, the pilgrims and the priests, the buying and selling of idols, offerings to the goddess, all the welter that existed somewhere near here 1,500 years ago.

The valley grew more dismal, more forlorn. Then, around a bend, I spotted a fading, weary café: the Café Sequana. A sign on an untended fence read Property of the City of Paris.

"Where may one find *les sources?*" I asked the cranky Madame inside, who had been sleeping on her hands.

She huffed at such stupidity: "*Par là!*" She inclined her head toward a cow pasture.

Through high, wet grass we plodded, wary of the few damp cows that looked up, startled. If they were irritated, well, so were we. Plosh, plosh. Then we spied it: a tasteless, pretentious grotto, a small basin with a few francs at its bottom, and, reclining upon a rock above, a statue of a fat, naked water-nymph (not Sequana, surely?) holding a cluster of grapes.

The holy Seine bubbled up through a grate under the enclosed edge of the monument, puddled into the pasture, and trickled away toward Paris.

I began to dance in the mud, jumping back and forth across the stream. "Evelyn, Evelyn! We did it! We have found *les sources de la Seine!*"

And Evelyn sighed, "*Pourquoi?*"

Searching for Cèpes

Susan Fox Rogers

Several days after it rains, *cèpes* sprout in the woods. Nut-brown, round-capped, and fleshy, this wild mushroom (*Boletus edulis*) pops out of the ground in late summer and fall throughout the world: Italians call them *porcini*, the Germans *steinpilz*, the Swedes *stensopp*.

Cèpe is a Gascon word, and in Gascony, a province in the southwest of France, good mushroom hunters are renowned. Capturing one of these prizes takes a keen eye, an inner map of the dips and curves of the valleys that run from the Pyrenees, and an intuition about which oak and chestnut trees might be sheltering this king of mushrooms. The experts *courent les bois* (run the woods), and seem to have sprung from the ground like the mushrooms themselves. The woods around Estampes, a village of fewer than two hundred people in the heart of the Gers, are rich with *cèpes*. This is where my mother was born.

During her childhood, my mother and her sister spent summers in Estampes, riding bikes, reading, and waiting for the daily mail that brought news from friends vacationing in their country homes, or from their American father, a journalist with the Paris edition of the *Chicago Tribune*. My grandmother, Jeanne Montégut, was also born in Estampes, and when she married an American, a Ragner, she promised her father she would never leave France. That promise was broken in 1941, when she and her family left France for the United States. There, my mother met my father, an American, at the University of Iowa, and married him.

Though no one dreamed of resuming life in Estampes, when I was growing up we visited every other summer. And now, from points around the globe, my family congregates in the old family house every July and August. As soon as we arrive, the first question from our neighbor Odette is: How long will you be here? And always—whether the answer is a week or two months—her response is the same: "*Mais ce n'est pas assez long.*" And she's right—my stays in Estampes are never long enough.

When I graduated from college in 1983 I was, finally, going to stay long enough: Estampes was to be my home. To most people it sounded romantic, but my parents questioned what I was going to do alone in the damp, bulky family house, and in a village so isolated I would have to bicycle six miles uphill to get the *Herald Tribune* (one day late) or *Libération*. I shrugged, secretly planning to live as the locals did. I had saved a little over a thousand dollars (this seemed a fortune to me) and it would stretch forever, I thought, since I would be growing my own vegetables, drinking milk from Stanis and Odette's cows, which slept in the barn next door, and eating eggs that their chickens had laid.

On a practical level it all seemed possible. Villagers had lived off the land for generations. And the house, once I'd removed the crucifixes that hung in each room, felt more like home than the house I had grown up in, in central Pennsylvania. It held generations of family in the form of books, linen, china, letters, and silver. In my hometown, State College, the name Rogers means little, but here in Estampes the name Montégut brings respect: My great-grandfather was the schoolteacher, and my grandmother a smart and commanding woman who received her *agrégation* (a PhD without a dissertation) in Bordeaux.

Despite these deep roots in the house and village, what I did not know when I arrived in 1983 was that none of my family had ever tromped through the surrounding woods of Estampes seeking the fleshy mushrooms that became, that summer, my obsession.

Stanis and Odette, like everyone in the village, lived off the land. While Odette tended the rabbits, chickens, and pigs, Stanis drove the tractor and milked the cows. At that time he still milked by hand, resting his cheek against the flank of one of his thirteen cows while speaking softly to her. Only I was saddened when they bought a milker in the mid-1980s.

I quickly fell into the rhythms of their lives, hoisting bales of hay and straw from small fields onto a cart, and every evening bringing the cows home from pasture along the narrow, grass-lined roads. I ate my noon meal in the cool of their kitchen.

"We'll hunt for *cèpes*," Stanis announced one day. After lunch we got into his old white Peugeot 303. The car barely had a floor, straw lingered on the seats, and the shocks should have been replaced long before. The driver's seat sagged, and Stanis drove hunched, like an old man, although he was not yet sixty.

He headed east toward the river Bouès, which has its source in the Pyrenees, about sixty miles south. The road soon became dirt and rock, leading past cow pastures and cornfields, and then finally to the woods that border the river. Lighting a cigarette, Stanis smiled at me, his sun-hardened face wrinkling so that his eyes disappeared into slits beneath his beret. Odette had just told me that he didn't smoke anymore.

Though Stanis, with his tan line cut into his upper arm and the beret that never left his head, appeared Gascon, he hailed from Poland. His black hair, dark eyes, and high cheekbones gave away his origins. A half dozen of his nine siblings, all Baczkowskis, had settled in and near Estampes. Strong and hard-working, and in every way a Gascon peasant, he drank local red wine for breakfast and punctuated his speech with *putain* and *con* (translation: whore and cunt). "*Ah, putain, il fait chaud,*" was his summer refrain. "*Ah, con, tu peux le dire,*" he agreed when I told him it was hot. Despite this, many still thought of him as a foreigner; the unwritten requirements of being local, *du pays,* were strict.

Stanis and I made an unusual couple. I topped him by a few inches and could not have looked more American with my wide shoulders, short brown hair, and open smile revealing teeth straightened by braces. Stanis was abrupt and often cantankerous, barking at Odette as they went about their daily chores. But with me he was almost always patient, and on Tuesdays I tagged along when he took a pig to the market fifteen miles away in Trie. We would leave at six in the morning, and by eight, the pig sold, we'd be standing at the bar in Trie, Stanis the center of attention with his *Américaine*. He'd drink wine and I'd drink café au lait, smiling at his friends from neighboring towns who winked at me while swapping information on pigs.

Stanis and I parked in the shade to avoid the midday heat and walked into the woods. In the cool darkness, leaves crunched underfoot. Stanis held his stick like a gun, slung over his shoulder. With the stick, carefully selected from a birch tree and trimmed smooth to perfection, he knocked at the ground and overturned leaves as if to ambush a mushroom, to surprise it into being there. It was also the stick he used to take the cows to pasture, to tap them on their haunches when they strayed or loitered too long by the side of the road, grazing on the rich green grass that sprouted there. Once I misplaced the stick, a gesture of carelessness that Stanis could not ignore; that was the only time he yelled at me. "*Ah, putain, c'est pas possible. Qu'est-ce que tu as fait?*" (What have you done?)

Stanis moved from tree to tree, abruptly lifting leaves. I tried to focus on my own search, but I wasn't sure where to look, or even *how* to look. So I watched Stanis as he poked at the earth. "There aren't any more mushrooms," Stanis concluded.

How could he be so sure so quickly? *"Pourquoi?"* I asked. There should have been mushrooms—everyone said the woods were full of them.

"It's not like the old days," he said.

He meant the days when only people from Estampes came to these woods. Now, people came from neighboring towns, from Tarbes forty-five minutes away, or from Auch, the home of the swashbuckling Musketeer d'Artagnan. They were foreigners. I wondered if Stanis realized how far I had come to hunt these mushrooms.

My grandmother liked Stanis, but she and several of my ancestors would have fainted over my friendship with him. He, after all, was a *paysan*, a peasant. My family was bourgeois, and it was important to them to maintain the distinction. Odette, who knows the history of our house and our family, the day and year everyone was born and died, tells stories of how my mother spent her summers reading books, and how my grandfather took leisurely strolls, perhaps picking a blackberry or two. They did not dirty their hands, did not go to market, bale hay—or hunt for mushrooms.

When we returned to the house, less than an hour after leaving, Odette stood in the doorway, her blue flowered dress framed by the white of their house, broom in hand. Her short, gray-white hair clung tightly to her scalp, damp from the heat. The last crumbs from our lunch were gone and her kitchen was all whiteness.

"*Alors?*" she asked.

"*Rien,*" we answered together. I tried to imitate Stanis's accent, rolling the "r" in the back of my throat, saying it with the confidence of someone from Estampes and with the irritation of a villager deprived of mushrooms that should rightfully have been hers.

My farming life grew: I seeded carrots and lettuce for late-summer crops. When the lettuce all bolted on the same day, I walked from plant to plant snapping off the heads; a milky fluid oozed from the stalks onto the ground. Stanis stood on the road, arms folded, and watched, unimpressed. It was clear to all that I was no farmer. So I turned my energy to home repair, painting the wooden shutters a rich caramel and the dining room a fresh yellow. I emptied cupboards, uncovering old *Life* magazines from the '30s and doctor's implements from the turn of the century. I polished the silver and washed the heavy linens of aunts long gone. I discovered *Les Misérables* in its original serialized edition, ten centimes per book, and read the series in the overly still evenings.

The house had originally belonged to a Doctor Sénat, whose only son, Ferdinand, died young. So the doctor gave the house to my grandmother. Various aunts had kept the kitchen spotless and cluttered the mantelpieces with photographs of themselves in elaborate dresses. They left piles of their crystal, silver, and china in the heavy wooden cabinets. In 1973, when the old aunts had all died, the house became ours to care for, clean out, and fix up.

While hanging my aunts' enormous bloomers to dry on a drooping cotton cord in the back field, I remembered our early visits, and how our neighbor, Marie Louise, bent and frail, would take our laundry and soap it up in the river Bouès. My jeans would return stiff and spiffy clean. I tried to imagine my aunts peeing in chamber pots and trotting to the outhouse that was replaced in 1978 with an indoor bathroom. They drew water from the stilled pump and heated it on a fire. But I reminded myself that the strenuous daily work had been left to maids or to local day workers. For a while, even, Odette had helped out one of my aunts, Madame Castay, who was confined to a wicker-bottomed wheelchair; she scolded Odette if she arrived late or did a job improperly. *"Tu sens le chien mouillé"* (You smell like a wet dog), she once told Odette, who did not forget the insult. Odette reminds me that my mother's family arrived from Paris with a maid, who slept on a fold-up bed under the staircase, and then hired a local helper as well. Until my parents took over, Odette had never been in our house except to work—to clean or to serve. Now she comes over for drinks, enjoying fruit juices and salted nuts while sitting in the quiet courtyard.

I walked alone through the woods near our house, looking for *cèpes*. I found mushroom after mushroom, buried beneath the leaves of oak trees. At each find, I felt a rush of excitement. I had figured out what to look for. Not color, but a shift from one shade of brown to another, from one texture to another, the smooth surface of the mushroom against the rough of the leaves. I bent slowly to pick my prizes, as if moving too quickly might make them vanish. I grasped the thick, off-white stems in my hand and dislodged the rootless fungus. Most were the size of a tennis ball; some were wormy, the flesh decomposing; others were turning olive brown on the underside, a sign they were past their prime. Most were solid, yellow-brown, or chestnut brown—perfect mushrooms.

Or so I thought. When I pressed my thumb into the spongelike underbelly of one, it turned an ominous purple, a sure sign that it was the poisonous cousin of the *cèpe*. I tested more; mushroom after mushroom came up foul. Refusing to let my disappointment get the better of me, I kept my poisonous loot anyway, the weight in the basket a comfort, a featherweight sense of accomplishment. But as I approached the village, I dropped them in a neat pile in the ditch by the side of the road.

Back at their house, Odette stood over the stove in the kitchen making blackberry jam from berries I had picked. When she saw my empty basket, she laughed, but clearly she felt sorry for me.

"Ah, *l'Américaine*," Stanis teased.

Yes, American and middle class, and that was why, I sensed, I could not find those mushrooms. Of course, anyone can hunt mushrooms, and the middle class do and did. But in Estampes it was the province of the *paysans*, those who *courent les bois*. And yet frustration lingered—did I not have a right to those mushrooms? In the house up the hill rested generations of family letters, books, and clothing; in the graveyard rested my great-grandfather and great-grandmother with my grandmother. Was I not enough *du pays* to find one lousy mushroom?

My obsession with the mushrooms had nothing to do with eating them. I didn't tell anyone this, but I don't like to eat *cèpes*. When the mushrooms are cleaned and sliced, they are then sautéed in duck or goose fat and they take on a slimy texture. That, coupled with the deep earthen taste, makes them a challenge for me to chew and swallow. My hunt had nothing to do with subsistence, or even with sport. What I wanted was to find a bagful of enormous mushrooms and bring them home and have Odette marvel at them, at me. I wanted her to tell everyone how I, too, could *courir les bois*. "Tomorrow Marie Claire will go with you," Odette said. "She has the eye."

"Yes, Marie Claire has the eye," Stanis confirmed, nodding his head and winking. *Elle court.* He had taken his seat at the end of the Formica kitchen table. In front of him was a crossword puzzle, half finished.

Marie Claire was one of Stanis's many nieces. She was a few years older than me, and an anomaly in the eyes of the village: over twenty-five and unmarried. *"C'est triste,"* Odette said, making it clear she thought Marie Claire would never find someone to marry who would want to live in Estampes. Marie Claire worked as a dental assistant in Trie but she was one of only a few who had figured out how to stay in Estampes without farming. The price was to remain single.

When Marie Claire appeared the next day just after lunch, I saw a French version of myself: a skinny young woman who kept in motion. We drove to the edge of town, not talking much except to comment on the heat of the day and the likelihood of finding *cèpes* after the rain of a few days before.

"It is prime mushrooming weather," she explained. "If we don't find something *nous sommes nulles.*"

She knew all the spots, had her special trees that always harbored new mushrooms. They were unknown to the outsiders who often picked mushrooms to sell to restaurants—or to Parisians for twice, or even four times, the money. "Parisian" to most in the village is synonymous with "rich." So is "American," but Marie Claire did not see me as an outsider; I felt as if I might be a cousin of hers visiting from out of town. In fact, the woods we entered belonged to a cousin of a cousin of hers. Everyone in the village is related in some way, but some cousins you talk to and some you don't; some let you mushroom on their land, and some do not.

Barely ten steps into the woods, she stopped. "Look here," she said. And I felt like a child at an Easter egg hunt. *Colder, warmer, warmer, colder.*

I finally saw the mushroom, nestled brown against brown, the rounded cap polished against the brittle leaves. *Texture, look for texture.* But this was just a piece, the edge of the cap. How had she seen it? She shrugged. *Comme ça.* Like that. It seemed that my ancestors had given me eyes good for reading books, not eyes for spotting *cèpes.*

We walked for hours, several paces apart, the only sound the crunch of leaves underfoot, or a tractor plowing a field in the distance. We spoke only when she found something. I would approach as she cleaned the small clumps of dirt from the rounded base. "*C'est joli*," I said, over and over, as if she had made the mushrooms herself. Marie Claire's dark eyes were focused, her gaze devoted.

At the end of the day, Marie Claire had a plastic bag full of mushrooms, some of them the size of a large softball. Later, at home, she took pictures of them—her trophies. I had that one mushroom Marie Claire had pointed me to, and when I showed it to Stanis and Odette, we all laughed. I didn't have the eye. It appeared that there was not one bit of mushrooming talent in my blood.

Still, I was willing to walk for days, to *courir*, as Marie Claire did. I wanted to bury myself in the woods to find those mushrooms, as if the woods were our house, and behind the oak and chestnut trees, I'd find not bloomers, walking canes, or weathered photographs, but an alternate history. My mushrooming motivation was transparent: I wanted to be a part of the village in this way, as none of my relatives had been.

My search continued, solo and with others. Alone, far in the woods, and far past the hope of finding a *cèpe*, I looked down and saw one. Cautiously, I stooped to pick it, pulling firmly so that the rounded base came out of the ground. I pressed my thumb into the fleshy underbelly and waited for it to turn purple; when it remained a soft white-brown shade, I tried again, pushing more firmly. I looked around, my loot in hand, as though there ought to be someone there to admire it.

I stood for a moment, trying to orient myself—I wasn't lost, but I wasn't sure how I had arrived at this point, deep in the woods. The sun dipped behind the hill as I turned, my plastic bag holding that one mushroom swinging at my side. A ravine paralleled my route, and I dropped into it. In the muddy, rocky banks another mushroom might lurk; my one had made me greedy for two. But before I could find another, the ravine ended, giving onto flat land. There were trees in every direction.

I continued to a dirt road, deeply rutted from tractors hauling firewood. I took the road, then realized that it headed north; I wanted to be walking south and east. Stanis would not get disoriented like this. Neither would Marie Claire.

Switching directions, I soon emerged on familiar territory. The land curved down to the main road that shot through town and straight south, where there appeared a faint outline, a pink-white glow from the mountains. In the passing beauty of late-afternoon light, the church steeple shone black. At the bottom of the hill, I faced the graveyard. Without hesitating I slipped the metal ring that held the rusted gate closed, and stepped onto the gravel paths that led to the tombstones, all carrying familiar names: Sénat, Lucantis, Langlade, Millas, Morlas, Claverie, Egran. Lightly touching my forehead, I made the sign of the cross.

Suddenly I was crying. Perhaps it was the immediacy of death—the still-blooming flowers, and in a corner, freshly turned dirt piled next to a glistening new tombstone. Or maybe it was the familiarity of the names: I had known so many of these people. I laid down my plastic bag and pulled the grass that grew at the edge of the family tomb. Dull, and solid gray, the tomb ran just longer than a person and rose like an uncomfortable granite bed, with a cross in relief on the top. I picked at the dense lichen that grew in the corners of the tomb, then ran my fingers along the names—Ragner, Montégut, Rogers—inscribed on the front.

My grandmother rested there, her ashes mingling with the bones of her father and mother. When we buried her in 1982, my sister Becky watched as the undertaker loosened the cement that sealed the front of the tomb and then pushed aside the bones to make room for her small box of ashes. Becky was upset at the sight of her great-grandparents' tibia bones knocking against each other, and at how the undertaker moved the remains without ceremony or piety. But they were just bones. He had to pick them up and move them. *You had to get your hands dirty.* We were all going to end up in the same place, bones or ashes resting in the earth, dirty hands or not.

A noise drew my attention. It was my plastic bag fluttering in the breeze. My one mushroom was not heavy enough to hold the bag to the ground.

Back home, I ate my mushroom—I had to—scrambled into eggs, their yolks orange-red.

Within the year, I left Estampes. Every year I return and walk the back roads, the same ones I followed with Stanis and Odette to take the cows to pasture. This past year I noticed metal signs tacked to trees at the entrance to the woods. They read: A permit is required to hunt mushrooms. Only locals are allowed in these woods. I will get my permit and search for *cèpes*.

A Change in Le Havre

Ginger Adams Otis

"Sue, this train is going to France!" I exclaimed to my friend with dismay. I reread the ticket. "We're going to have to spend the night there, and that's my birthday. That's the one day I told you I did not want to be in France!"

"Look, it won't be that bad," Sue said, in a vain attempt to calm me down.

Up until this moment, our trip had been perfect. Armed with budget guidebooks, Sue and I had been happily traveling for six weeks, from North Africa up the Iberian coast, through Barcelona, skirting the French Riviera, into Italy, to Athens, Geneva, Austria, and Germany. Now we were headed to Ireland, and it turned out, to my chagrin, that this overnight train from Berlin required a change of trains—in Paris.

"At least we don't have to stay in Paris," Sue cajoled, seeing my exasperation. "We'll arrive late in Le Havre, sleep well, wake up, have breakfast, and be on our way. And we'll just pretend your birthday didn't happen until we get to Ireland."

I had not always been so averse to France. But at the tender age of sixteen, during a class trip to Paris, I had been exposed to a nearly lethal dose of Parisian chic. Insults had rained down upon my group of well-fed and badly dressed American girls from all quarters. The worst came on the night we climbed to Sacré-Coeur in Montmartre; I was singled out by a caricaturist who took great delight in lampooning me on paper. I sat obediently as he sketched, never suspecting he was casting me as a plump, countrified Pippi Longstocking. Passersby gathered around, snickering, as he worked. I had never recovered from the traumatic week.

"Easy for you to say," I said, haunted by the image of Madame Descouteaux, my high school chaperone, so outré and confident back in New Hampshire, who'd done nothing to shield me from that long-ago nightmare in Paris. What chance would I have in fashion-obsessed France today, emerging from an overnight train trip wearing sweatpants, with lank hair and a bulky backpack? When the time came to switch in Paris, I pulled my hood up and mutely followed Sue around as she tried to locate our local train. Not until we were safely heading away from Gare du Nord did I emerge from my woolen cocoon.

We arrived in Le Havre at close to midnight on one of the coldest, foulest nights I'd seen in a long time. In the train station, Sue put down her pack and dug out her guidebook. "We've got two options," she said. "One place that is supposed to be a 'decent' budget option, that looks like it will be farther away, or a place around the corner that's described as 'basic.' Which do you want?"

While I debated, the wind outside began to pick up. An empty garbage can came tumbling out of nowhere and slammed against the main terminal door, almost shattering the glass. "Let's go for the one that's closest," I said.

We pulled on our yellow slickers and stepped out into the storm. The mixture of snow and freezing rain came down hard, and occasional sudden bursts of wind sent stinging pellets right into our faces.

During the long train ride, I had flipped through the pages on Le Havre in the guidebook, and I knew it had once been a wealthy shipping port with an impressive history—Henry V's rousing speech about going "once more into the breach, dear friends" supposedly happened here. But the city had been bombed into near oblivion during World War II and had never really recovered. Even on a terrifically windy night, the stench of factory pollution hung heavy in the air. With heads bent, we trudged past empty warehouses and the occasional piece of heavy machinery.

The ten-minute walk seemed interminable, and I'd begun to fear that we had taken a wrong turn when Sue pointed toward a porch light set a few feet back from the road. We climbed the sagging steps and knocked on the front door, then entered and shut the door firmly against the howling wind.

Our entrance silenced a room that had been buzzing with voices. Ten pairs of thickly lashed, almond-shaped eyes turned our way. Squinting against the bright lights that bounced off warm orange walls, I saw a group of young men lounging around a crackling fire.

"*Comment je peux vous aider?*" one of the men asked, stepping forward and walking behind the small check-in desk. "Are you lost?"

"We're looking for this hotel," I said, fumbling with wet hands for the guidebook. "Is this the right place?" I asked nervously.

The man nodded and waved an elegant finger at the sign on the desk that read L'Hôtel Le Havre. "We are a hotel," he said, "but we rarely lodge women." He had a quiet voice that shouldn't have sounded at all sinister.

The ten men stealing occasional glances at us didn't seem unfriendly, but they kept their distance, looking down rather than at us and whispering in Arabic.

"At this hour you shouldn't be walking the streets of Le Havre," said the young man at the desk, who apparently functioned as the night clerk. "I will check you in."

I wasn't sure how Sue felt, but I was decidedly uncomfortable. If we'd been standing in a bar surrounded by men from a different country and speaking a different language, I don't think I would have minded. But we were going to sleep among them.

"Perhaps we should try the other hotel," I stammered, and heard Sue's faint agreement. The clerk, not at all put out, extended his hand for my guidebook and pointed to the second budget listing.

When I nodded, he dialed the number and chatted in rapid-fire French to someone on the other end.

He hung up and said apologetically, "The hotel is full for the night. You will have to stay here."

Sue stepped up beside me and gave me a look that said, "No matter what happens, we stick together, right?"

I tacitly agreed and said, "OK, we'd like one room, please. We'll stay together."

"I'm sorry," said the clerk. "We only have single rooms. You can stay right next to each other, but there are no double rooms available."

Sue and I exchanged wary glances. The rain gusted outside and cold air brushed against our ankles as we stood by the door.

"Look," I said firmly to the clerk. "We want to stay together, in the same room. I don't care if you have to bring a second bed in. But we aren't separating."

The clerk smiled, flashing bright white teeth against a dark mustache. "The rooms are very small and narrow. There is room for one bed only. I will put you on the part of the second floor that is empty. You will be the only two guests in that section. But you can't share a room."

All I wanted was a warm shower and a good night's sleep on something that didn't shimmy and shake all night long. I looked at Sue and nodded my head and the clerk cleared his throat happily.

"Will you now please give me your passports and sign in?" he asked politely. Despite several weeks of traveling around Europe, I still hadn't gotten used to handing over my passport at check-in, and tonight this custom seemed more ominous than ever. Reluctantly, we handed over our identification.

"This way, please," said the young man, and he led us through the living room, where his friends stood back to let us pass, then up a shaky staircase. The second floor was surprisingly large, with dark empty hallways stretching away on either side of the stairs. The clerk turned to the right and brought us all the way to the end of the hall.

"Your room is here," he said to Sue, giving her the key to the second door from the end, "and your room is right next door," he said to me. "The bathroom is here on the right—we are sorry but there is no door for it at this time. The showers are free and you will find plenty of hot water. If you need me, you'll have to come downstairs. There are no phones."

He bid us goodnight and walked away.

Each room contained one small dresser and one tiny bed. I could stand in the middle and touch both walls with my fingertips. The enforced separation still made us feel more vulnerable than we would have liked, but at least we *were* very close to each other. The biggest problem now was the doorless bathroom, but we soon discovered that the shower stalls were set in such a way as to be invisible from the hallway. Sue guarded the doorway while I got ready for bed, then I did the same for her. Finally, we turned out the lights.

"If you need anything, knock on the wall," I said to her before we parted in the hallway. "And if you hear me knocking, start screaming as loud as you can."

The faint murmur of laughter and chatter drifted up the stairwell from the living room. Sue hesitated.

"Let's push the dressers against the doors," she said.

For the next minute, the sound of scraping furniture filled the halls, and must have echoed through the whole drafty house. When we were done, I felt slightly better. I fell asleep around 2:00 A.M., clutching my travel guide, which was the bulkiest thing I had, in case I needed a weapon to smash over someone's head.

Some hours later, a noise awakened me. The dark velvet drapes kept out light, and I didn't know how long I'd been asleep. I lay tensely in bed and listened hard. "Sue?" I whispered loudly. "Are you awake?" No answer. I rolled closer to the wall and lightly tapped on it. "Sue," I repeated. "Are you OK?" Still no answer.

I rolled onto my back and lay still. There was nothing but silence around me and I was just getting ready to close my eyes again when something jolted me upright in bed. Footsteps moved down the hallway and stopped near my door, followed by the sound of a knob turning. I kicked the covers off my bed and grabbed my book. I waited, hand on the dresser blocking the door, and tried to quiet my breathing.

I heard a low rumble, like someone talking—Arabic, I thought— and then, unmistakably, a stifled giggle. Sue needed my help! I wrestled the empty dresser aside and wrenched open the door, travel guidebook at the ready.

Ten male voices shouted at once. "Surprise!"

"Happy birthday!" Sue yelled, and then doubled over with laughter. "You should see what you look like," she gasped.

The same young clerk who had checked us in the night before held a tray with a croissant, orange juice, and a single flower on it. "We saw on your passport that today is your birthday," he said, and the smile that had seemed sinister last night suddenly seemed soft and lovely. "We were going to leave this tray at your door without disturbing you, but we woke up your friend. She convinced us that you would like the surprise."

I looked at him and his friends, speechless and shamefaced. As my blush of surprise turned into an embarrassed red, the young men began to chuckle loudly, reliving my look of fear and bewilderment upon opening the door. Some words were in French, others in Arabic, but I knew these men were clearly my *friends*. Sue and I asked if we could bring the breakfast tray downstairs and join them. Ali, previously known as the clerk, took my tray while we washed and dressed. Within ten minutes we were all assembled around a big mahogany table in the otherwise dreary dining room. Over piping hot café au lait and delicious fresh fruit, I learned that most of the men came from Morocco and were in France to study. They ranged in age from eighteen to thirty-five and had chosen Le Havre because it was inexpensive. When they weren't studying, they provided cheap labor at the innumerable construction sites around town.

"Don't you miss home?" I asked to the table in general, but keeping my eyes on Mohammed. He was the oldest of the group and had emigrated with all three of his younger brothers, who also lived in the hotel/boarding house. Most of the men seemed to have adjusted to living far from home, but I sensed that Mohammed, perhaps bearing the weight of surrogate parenthood, struggled the most.

"Of course," he said, after the others had all shrugged their shoulders. "This is not our culture and we feel the difference every day. But this is where the opportunities are for us."

"But don't you find the French mean to foreigners?" I pushed. I launched into my horror story from high school, exaggerating a bit for dramatic effect. Instead of commiserating, to my surprise, they all laughed. Ali, whose manners were so gentlemanly as to be almost unreal, coughed repeatedly to cover up his stifled laughter, but the others did little to hide their amusement. Even Mohammed couldn't keep a straight face.

"Well, yes," Mohammed said, collecting himself at the end of my tale. "But what happens in Paris doesn't necessarily happen in the rest of France. Of course we have sometimes been treated like outsiders by the French. Why do you think we prefer to live together? But there are marvelous things here, things we can't learn in our country, and things you can't learn in your country either, *n'est-ce pas?*" I nodded reluctantly, still too stubborn to fully admit I might be wrong in holding onto five-year-old grudges.

"And besides," added Ali, leaning forward with a teasing look, "most of us are now French citizens, although we aren't what most people really think of as French. And we haven't treated you badly, have we?" I was deeply touched by his bit of ambassadorial defense of the French, especially since I knew colonial prejudices still abounded.

I mutely shook my head, and let the subject drop. Soon it was time to head for the docks and find our boat to Ireland. Ali took a rare trip away from the front desk to accompany us, and several of our newfound friends came, too. Mohammed, claiming a prior commitment, gave us two warm handshakes and a smile goodbye. We got on the boat with plenty of time to spare, and with the exception of a sudden storm that kept us hovering off the Irish coast for several hours, all went as planned.

I never saw those men again, and on a recent trip to Le Havre I discovered that the hotel had long since been torn down. I imagine the cozy group I met almost fifteen years ago has scattered far and wide, but I think of them often. Sitting in that dingy dining room surrounded by a group of Moroccan students was the first time I had felt welcome in France, and although Mohammed and Ali's words didn't immediately change my opinion about the country, they wedged an opening in me.

That experience marked the beginning of what has become a love affair with France, for without that night in Le Havre, I probably never would have known the gorgeous serenity of the Pyrenees, the deep, primal forest of Alsace, the salty tang of Marseilles. If not for those young Moroccan men, I might have spent my life changing trains in Paris but never getting off.

Comfort Me with Apples

Ruth Reichl

When I told my mother that I was planning a trip to France, she was immediately suspicious. "Is that food editor of yours going to be there?" she demanded.

"He has nothing to do with it," I replied with as much dignity as I could muster. "He doesn't even know I'm going."

"But he will be there," she said.

"Yes," I replied in a very small voice. "He will."

"PussyCat," she said, "you're asking for trouble."

I certainly did not need her to tell me that. But ten minutes after Doug* had called to say that his wind tent was progressing more slowly than he had anticipated and he would be in Omaha at least two more weeks, my friend Béatrice called from Paris. Her apartment in the Sixth Arrondissement was empty, and it was mine

* the author's husband

if I wanted it. I took this to be a sign from heaven. Within minutes I had found a student charter flight to London and invented an assignment.

I took the boat train from London to Paris, sitting up all night with the scruffy kids with knapsacks and high hopes. It all felt comfortingly familiar—the dim light, the furtive departure from Dover, the French douaniers at Calais stamping their feet in the early-morning cold. And then I was on a train speeding through the gray countryside and everyone around me was speaking French. For a moment I remembered the terrible homesickness I had felt in my first years at French boarding school, and a great wave of loneliness swept over me. What did I think I was doing? My mother's voice was in my ear, suddenly very loud. "People don't behave this way," she said disapprovingly. Before I could stop her, she went on. "It will serve you right if that food editor won't even see you. And then what will you do, Miss Smarty Pants, all by yourself in Paris?"

I didn't have an answer. So I drew the shabby silver-wolf coat from Value Village around my shoulders and stared out the window, wishing I were in Berkeley, where it was sunny and I was not alone.

It was a cold, misty day, and as I stepped onto the platform at the Gare du Nord the train coughed up clouds of vapor, which enveloped me in a man-made fog. I looked up, and the black train hunched its back like a malevolent cat and hissed angrily at me. It was such an unfriendly sound that it suddenly hit me that I had only an address and Béatrice's assurance that she had written a note to the concierge. A sudden vision materialized: the concierge, looking me up and down and dismissing me with a curt, "Je n'en sais rien. On ne m'avait rien dit. Au revoir, mademoiselle." I looked down at my shoes and wished, once again, that I had thought to polish them.

The Métro was filled with people looking very purposeful, on their way to work. Watching them reading their papers and scurrying off to their jobs made me feel foreign, aimless, and alone; by the time I reached my stop I was so homesick I could barely drag myself from the train. I tried to shake myself out of the mood; I knew it was ridiculous. And then I climbed out into the air and started searching for the rue Auguste Comte, a bit startled by the elegance of the neighborhood.

Béatrice lived in a pale Beaux-Arts beauty of a building, with baroque curves and graceful wrought-iron balconies. I patted my hair, wishing it looked less like a rat's nest, and bit my lips to give them color before pushing open the huge wooden door into the entryway.

"Vous désirez?" the concierge inquired. Her voice was like ice. She was exactly what I had expected: a small, officious woman with short, sensible black hair and shapeless, colorless clothes. My French deserted me completely, and I stammered in English, "I am the friend of Béatrice du Croix. I will be staying in her apartment?"

She fumbled for her glasses and peered at me. "Je ne parle pas anglais," she said shortly, and turned to go.

"Je m'excuse," I said quickly, a flood of French coming to my rescue. "Le voyage était si fatigant. Je suis l'amie de Béatrice du Croix. Nous nous connaissions a l'école. Elle m'avait gracieusement offert son appartement."

"Elle parle!" said the concierge sarcastically. She did not encourage me to continue.

"On ne vous a rien dit sur moi?" I continued, a bit desperately. Already I saw myself on the street.

"Oui, mademoiselle," she finally conceded. She went to a desk, pulled out a large iron key, and handed it to me. She sniffed. "Troisième étage. Vous avez deux semaines. Au revoir." And she shut the door, leaving me in the blackness of the hall.

"Welcome to France," I muttered as I pressed the light for the landing. It sputtered reluctantly on, and I started the climb.

But once I had shut the door behind me, none of that mattered. It was a wonderful apartment, filled with light even on this gray day. I went to the window and looked out over the Luxembourg Gardens. And then I put my clothes into the beautiful eighteenth-century carved wooden armoire, climbed into the enormous sleigh bed covered with embroidered linen sheets, and fell fast asleep.

I woke up ravenous and went to explore the tiny Parisian kitchen. The refrigerator was a little box beneath a marble counter, but when I opened it I found bottled water, a few gnarled apples that looked like windfalls, a package of butter, a wedge of Chaource, and three bottles of Pouilly-Fumé. Two cracked blue bowls held brown eggs and walnuts, still in the shell. An ancient heel of bread sat on the counter, surrounded by bowls of spices, olive oil, vinegar, and a couple of bottles of vin ordinaire. This would certainly do.

I sliced the bread as thinly as I could and toasted it to make crackers. I put the cheese on a plate, surrounded it with sliced apples, and made myself an omelette. Then I poured myself a glass of wine and sat eating my good French omelette and my cheese and crackers, thinking that I was being a guest to myself and feeling very much like M. F. K. Fisher.

I piled the dishes into the sink and went to draw a bath in the enormous clawfoot tub. I found some crystals in a big glass, and when I sprinkled them into the water the tub began to fill with mounds of white bubbles. I poured myself another glass of wine and stepped into the bath. For a long time I lay there in the clean steam, feeling my body relax in the warmth. I would spend the afternoon at the Louvre.

Wrapped in towels, I wandered back into the bedroom and noticed the phone. It was an enameled white antique, perfect for calling your lover. I stared at it as I considered what to say to Colman. I lay back on the lacy sheets and down pillows. Somewhere out in the Gardens someone was playing a flute, and I followed the thread of music. There was plenty of time; lulled by Mozart and the featherbed, I drifted off to sleep.

It was dark when I woke up, and I was momentarily disoriented. What time was it? Without stopping to consider what I was doing, I reached for the phone and called Colman's hotel.

Waiting for the desk to connect me with his room, I panicked and hung up. My heart was thumping loudly in my chest. What if he was not alone? What if he wouldn't see me? I felt vulnerable and foolish and frightened, and by the time I got the courage to call back my hands were shaking.

Then his deep voice was in my ear and it went through me like a shock. "Where are you?" he asked.

"In Paris," I said.

"What are you doing here?" he demanded. He sounded irritated.

"Visiting friends," I answered.

"Is Doug with you?"

"No, I'm alone."

"Well," he said, considering, "we should get together sometime. But I was just on my way out to meet someone for dinner. Why don't you give me your number, and I'll call you in the next few days?"

I gave him my number, and he hung up. I wished I could snatch the call back. The days stretched out, empty, before me. Ten days was a long time. Why had I come? Maybe I could find an earlier plane home.

I burrowed into the pillows, ready to escape back into sleep. In the morning I would make a program, keep myself busy. I'd go to Beaubourg, spend a day at the Louvre, wander through the market on the rue du Cherche-Midi. If Colman called, I'd have lots to tell him. . . .

But what if he called tomorrow? I had never had a fancy meal by myself. I wasn't even hungry. But Colman would not waste his time in Paris making omelettes. What would he do? He would probably go to Taillevent or Tour d'Argent and eat a ten-course meal capped off with cognac and a fat cigar. Well, if he could do it, so could I; I was not going to tell him I had fasted on my first night in Paris.

Taillevent and Tour d'Argent were booked, but Guy Savoy was happy to provide a table for a single cover. How soon could I be there?

On the Métro I eavesdropped on my neighbors, trying to fix the sound of French in my ear. I did not want to seem like a tourist in the restaurant. When I arrived I said my name as carefully as possible, hoping that they would not know I was American. The maître d'hôtel seated me at a small table near the bar and asked if I would like an aperitif.

"Une coupe de champagne," I heard myself saying, to my surprise. He went to get it, returning with a little dish of salted, buttered nuts, tiny puffs of warm cheese gougères, and the menu.

I asked for the wine list as well, and the captain looked pleased with me. He returned, and we gravely discussed the possibilities for the evening. It took us fifteen minutes to arrive at a decision, but when we were done he assured me that I would be very content with my meal.

Though uninvited, my mother appeared with the first course. "Is this how you will spend the next ten days?" she inquired. "Eating absurdly expensive food all by yourself? Trying to impress waiters? Where will the money come from?"

"Be quiet, please," I said. "I'm busy. I want to remember every detail of this soup." I described it for myself, the cream, the truffles, the faintly nutty flavor that could only be sherry.

"He won't call anyway," she said, meanly I thought. I ordered a half bottle of Chassagne-Montrachet to go with the terrine de poisson and tried to describe the captain's demeanor as he served it. "When I came in," I told my phantom mother, "he thought to himself, Oh, a woman, she'll have the salad and some plain fish, and he was sorry he had taken the reservation. But I have turned out to be someone who likes to eat, and now he is a happy man."

"You're not going to order more wine, are you?" she asked with some alarm.

"Try me," I said, ordering a half bottle of '70 Palmer. Mom looked at the price and was scandalized, but the captain looked at me with serious interest and leaned in to ask how I liked it. I took one sip and thought how there is nothing, really nothing, like great wine. Mom just faded, like the Cheshire cat, as I began to describe the taste of the special lamb raised on the salt marshes of the Landes to myself. And to Colman. I was not lonely.

I had dacquoise for dessert, thinking of Los Angeles, and then, just because it seemed sporting, I ordered cognac with my coffee.

The room was practically empty now, but my captain urged me to have another glass of cognac as he set down the petits fours and macaroons and chocolates. I was sated and sleepy, however, and wanted nothing so much as to be in bed. "Our driver will take you home," said the captain as I paid the (enormous) bill. I added another hundred francs to the tip; it was still cheaper than a taxi.

I barely remember walking up the stairs, and I don't remember taking off my clothes or getting into bed. But when the phone's irritating beeping began to sound, that is where I was. I groped for the receiver, knocking the phone off the stand as I did so.

"Bonjour!" said Colman's voice in my ear. "Tu dormais?"

"Yes," I said, "I *was* asleep."

"Well, you're wasting your time in Paris. Get up. Get out. Come meet me for coffee."

"What time is it?" I asked.

"Time to get up," he said. "It's nine. Meet me in half an hour at the café at the foot of the boulevard Saint-Michel, just before the bridge. It's called Le Départ. I'll be there at nine-thirty."

I thought you were busy.

I can't possibly be there in half an hour.

You can't just snap your fingers.

I contemplated saying all those things, but what I really said was "Okay."

As soon as I hung up, I began to worry. Why had he called now? I knew that he was going to tell me that I should not have come, that he did not want to see me. It was like him to do it in person instead of on the phone. And to get it out of the way.

Well, I wasn't going to make it easy for him. I took my time, changed my clothes three times, wanting to make him regret what he was about to lose. I put on my green velvet skirt and a purple silk blouse, and then I changed it for a pair of plain black pants and then went back to velvet. Was this best? I didn't know, but now I was so late that I threw on the silver wolf and left.

Colman was sitting at a table by himself, tapping his paper irritably against the table. He stopped in mid-tap when he saw me and just looked up, without saying anything. I had planned to shake his hand, but instead I just sat down across from him and stared.

He looked wonderful in Paris. His hair was very black, and in his good clothes he looked like neither a Frenchman nor a tourist but some prosperous cosmopolitan who was at home in the world.

"Café?" he asked. I nodded. "Un crème," he said to the waiter; his accent wasn't bad, but it was clear he was not French. For the first time in my life I was glad my mother had sent me off to that French school. Just to show off, I said to the waiter, "Je voudrais aussi une tartine," because the words are hard for an American to pronounce correctly.

"Why is everybody ordering bread and butter this morning?" the waiter wondered in French. "I haven't sold a croissant."

"Oh," I replied, "it's the weather. Some days are just bread-and-butter days."

Colman seemed impressed by the exchange.

The coffee was just bitter enough. The bread, a skinny ficelle, crackled when I bit into the crust. The crumb was white and soft, and the butter was cold and sweet against it. "This is why I came," I said to Colman, and for that moment I meant it. "It's like having France in my mouth. If I stay away too long I forget the flavor."

Colman leaned across the table and took both my hands in his. "I'm so glad you're here," he said. "How long are you staying?"

"Ten days," I said.

"Well, we have to make them count."

I had clearly said the right thing.

My Paris was uncomfortable pensions on the outskirts of town, cheap meals that started with watery soup and ended with watery flan. It was always being cold. It was hours peering through the gloom of the badly lighted Louvre.

Colman's Paris was not mine.

He liked to start the day by strolling through the flower market and listening to the birds. Every morning he woke me with fresh flowers. Then he took me to Ladurée for coffee and croissants and we sat there, beneath the ancient paintings of nymphs and angels, bantering with the waitresses in their black dresses and white aprons. After three days we were regulars, and they didn't even ask what we wanted, but simply put out the pots of coffee and hot milk, and the plates of croissants.

He showed me streets I had never seen before and small, out-of-the-way museums. He took me to the cemetery and we danced around Proust's tomb, and afterward we went to Le Petit Zinc and ate platters of claires and spéciales washed down with a cold, crisp Sancerre. We walked along the Seine in the damp November air, and when my feet got cold he insisted on taking me to the nearest shop to buy me a pair of boots.

"But I've never spent two hundred dollars on a pair of boots," I protested, looking at the soft maroon leather he'd picked out.

"And you aren't now," he said.

"It's so extravagant," I protested.

"But do you like them?" he wanted to know. And of course I did.

Colman never considered the price. Of anything. He bought first-class tickets for the Métro and front-row seats for the Opéra. At night, walking along Saint-Michel, we went in and out of jazz clubs and he introduced me to the joys of La Vieille Prune. I loved the way it tasted, like gentle cognac.

"That first day," I said one night, after my third Prune, "you were going to tell me to go away. Weren't you?"

Colman looked down at me. "Was I?" he asked. "I don't remember." It wasn't like him to be clumsy, and I had a fleeting thought that there might have been another woman. If there was, I didn't want to know about it. "Besides," he said, catching himself, "that was a different time. It was before we had Paris."

"You think these things happen," I wrote one night in my journal as Colman lay in the other room, sleeping. He, no surprise, had not just a room but a suite. "And of course they do—sometimes—but never to you. Or you think that when they do you'll be too dumb to recognize it. But there it is, it's actually happening, and even I'm not so stupid that I don't enjoy every second. Both of us keep pinching ourselves. Is this really taking place?"

I watched us as if we were strangers, kissing and laughing on the Métro, incapable of keeping our hands off each other. I envied us, even as I lived it. We were the people everyone smiles at. It wouldn't last. This was the least sensible thing I had ever done in my life.

"Wear your best dress tonight," said Colman.

"Where are we going?"

"You'll see."

He took me the long way round, to get me lost, and then he made me close my eyes for the last few blocks. When I opened them we were standing in front of Tour d'Argent. "This is where we are dining."

"My first three-star restaurant," I said. And for a moment I thought what it would be like to go to a three-star restaurant with Doug. I was a restaurant critic, but I was still green enough that fancy places made me nervous. If I were with Doug we would both be embarrassed, and we'd get the worst table in the house and spend the whole night worrying about how much money we were spending.

But Colman had no shame. He gave his name at the front and the owner rushed up to shake his hand and lead us to a table by the window. "My nephew told me to take very good care of you," he said as he pulled out the chair. "Is that chef he has at Ma Maison really as good as he says?"

Colman nodded. "Better," he said.

"Well," said Monsieur Terrail, "we'll have to see if we can't impress you even more than he does." He opened a bottle of Krug

'66 and poured us each a glass. Then he disappeared. Colman raised his glass and suddenly I saw, through the bubbles, Notre Dame flooded with silvery light just across the Seine.

Dinner was a dance. Colman and Monsieur Terrail were moving in perfect time to the music, and I floated along between them as they dipped and swayed. What would we drink with the foie gras frais? Colman thought perhaps a Meursault, an older one. Ah yes, Monsieur Terrail was in perfect agreement; it was a fine thing, he thought, to have such a sympathetic guest. The wine would be very nice, did he not agree, with the brouillade aux truffes?

The foie grass was molten velvet in my mouth, and when I took a sip of wine the flavor became even more intense, richer and rounder than it already was. Colman looked at me, and I felt the thrill all the way down to my fingertips. I understood, for the first time ever, why those turn-of-the-century restaurants had private rooms with velvet couches. I would have liked a couch.

The scrambled eggs with truffles were even better than the foie gras. Minutes earlier I would not have thought it possible. Each forkful was like biting off a piece of the sun. It was like musk and light, all at once, and suddenly I burst out, "This is what I always imagined sex would taste like."

Colman put back his head and roared. "Being with you," he said, "is just like being by myself. Only better." And he picked up my hand, across the table, and kissed it.

Monsieur Terrail was back now, lighting a candle. He crooned a little as he decanted the wine, and I knew it must be very, very good.

"What is it?" I whispered.

"Oh," said Colman. "A Petit-Village from my birth year." He looked a bit smug and said, "You know, '45 was a very good year."

"And '48?" I asked.

"Not as good," he said. And then, quickly, "But a very good year for women."

I thought, briefly, of what the world was like when the wine was put into the bottle. Paris was being liberated; there was dancing in the streets. I imagined I could taste all that. Afterward there was sorbet and framboises Chantilly and an ancient cognac. "This is probably costing more than I make in a year," I said to Colman.

"Probably," he said. "You know, I was thinking that tomorrow we could take the train to Boyer for lunch. It's only got two stars, but it will probably get its third this year. I want you to taste la fameuse truffe en croûte."

We were very drunk walking back to his hotel, and I put my head on his chest as we walked, listening to his deep, wonderful voice resonating through his coat. I wanted the night to never end.

We did go to Boyer the next day, where we drank antique Roederer champagne from 1911. "I hope I'm this vibrant when I'm sixty-seven," said Colman. There was a kind of magic to champagne that old, a wine bottled before automobiles or airplanes or either of the major wars. A wine bottled before women had the vote. Watching the liquid come sparkling into my glass, I thought of all the years it had been waiting in that dark bottle, what a different world it was emerging into. I was drinking history; I liked the taste.

The whole truffle was incredible too; it looked like a lump of coal wrapped up in pastry. The crust was flaky, but once I got through I hit the truffle, which tasted the way a forest smells in autumn when the leaves are turning colors and someone, far off, is burning them.

Colman watched as I ate; I could feel my cheeks get flushed. "I always thought truffles were overrated," I said. "I had no idea. Thank you."

He took my hand, caressed it. "Tomorrow," he said, "I have another surprise." There was an odd look on his face, dreamy and wistful. "I am going to introduce you to someone very special."

I couldn't imagine who it might be.

A marcassin, the hide of a young wild boar, was stretched across the door of the restaurant we were approaching. "You don't see that much anymore," said Colman. "But this is an old-fashioned bistro, the real thing."

"Chez Isadore," I read, looking at the writing above the boar's prickly speckled fur. "Is it Isadore I'm here to meet?"

"No," he said. He led me inside, where it was warm and steamy and smelled like butter, onions, wine, and meat. The room was filled with solid people, planted firmly at their tables. A man in a long white apron, platters stacked up his arms, whirled through the room, bantering as he delivered food. "Monsieur Colman!" he cried joyfully when he spotted us. He cocked his head and looked quizzically at me. "Is this . . . ?" he asked. Colman shook his head, almost imperceptibly, and then quickly said, "This is my good friend Ruth, from California."

With a puzzled look on his face, Isadore took my hand politely. "Monsieur awaits you," he said, leading us to a large table beneath the mirror in the corner.

A short, quite stout older man with a bald, shiny head was sitting there reading a newspaper. He beckoned happily when he saw us— he had beautiful hands—and stood up, painfully, as we approached. He looked exactly the way I have always imagined A. J. Liebling, which I found oddly disconcerting.

The man embraced Colman as well as he could, given that he was half his size. He showered upon him one of those loving looks usually reserved for one's children, and I wondered if he might be Colman's father. I thought he had told me that his parents were dead.

"So this is why we have seen so little of you." The man looked me up and down, very frankly, and I was a little embarrassed by the scrutiny. "Je m'appelle Claude," he said, taking my hand. Then he turned to Colman and said—reproachfully, I thought—"Pepita has missed you."

"How is she?" asked Colman.

He sighed. "Fragile, I am afraid. But come, what am I thinking of? Let us sit down. I have taken the liberty of ordering. Do you mind?"

Even dining with him was the way I had always imagined a meal with A. J. Liebling. We were no sooner seated than Isadore arrived with trays of oysters—spéciales and claires—balanced on each arm. He set them on the table—four of them!—and poured glasses of Sancerre. "Never stint on oysters," said Claude. "It takes away the pleasure." He picked up an oyster, gave it a solid squeeze of lemon, and raised it to his mouth. "Ah," he said when he had downed it. "They are excellent! We must have more." He beckoned Isadore to bring another platter.

As he ate he asked questions. Where was I from, why was I here, what had I thought of Boyer? He asked about my family, my work, my hopes. Before the oysters were half gone he had collected an entire dossier on me. "Are you a reporter?" I asked, taken aback by the intensity of the interview.

"Bravo, ma fille!" he said. "I was, for more than fifty years, before I retired. That is how I met Colman's family. I was sent to California when he was a small boy. Pepita and I could never have children, and so I have always thought of Colman as a little bit my own. Now we will have some grilled sardines; Isadore says they are excellent today, and he has never misled me." He turned to Colman. "Tell me, shall we have a different wine?"

"I was thinking of Burgundy with the sardines," said Colman, who always sped through the whites in his rush to the reds.

"My sentiments precisely," said Claude. "I have trained you well."

Then there was a roast partridge with an enormous pile of crisp, hot frites. It tasted wild and funky, with that high, almost electric note you find only in birds that have never been caged. "The secret," said Claude, "is in hanging the birds long enough. When I was a boy every bistro in Paris knew how to hang its meat, but Isadore is one of the last of the breed. In other restaurants partridge is no better than chicken. Worse, in fact; it's dry chicken."

Colman was saying very little, just watching the interchange between this wonderfully crusty old Frenchman and me. I thought, from the expression on his face, that I was doing pretty well. Still, when Isadore arrived with a bottle of Bordeaux and began decanting it, I felt momentary panic. More?

"The marcassin, of course," said Claude. "You must try it. Marcassin is disappearing in France; in ten more years it will be gone." I took a bite and words like "morne," "farouche," and "goût de terroir" came leaping to my lips. I was a little drunk, and Colman and Claude were egging me on.

When the boar was gone there was still wine in the bottle. "A pity to waste this, don't you think?" asked Claude, summoning Isadore to the table. The room was starting to empty out of patrons and fill up with the scent of cigars. It was so much like going back sixty years to that fantasy Paris of the twenties that I was almost in tears. I wished I were wearing an ankle-length black skirt instead of pants, and a white lace blouse. "Do you have a piece of cheese hidden away, a piece of cheese that will do this Pauillac justice?" asked Claude.

Isadore considered. "Bien sûr," he said. "I think perhaps the aged Gouda would do very well. I have had it in the cellar for two years, and it has a roundness the wine will like." He rushed off to fetch it, and Colman excused himself.

"Well, ma fille," said Claude when we were alone. "How did you come to be in Paris?"

"Oh," I said flippantly, "I followed Colman here."

"He didn't invite you?" he asked gleefully. Why was he so happy about this? Did he enjoy the notion of women throwing themselves at his adopted son?

"No," I said, "he didn't invite me. But I hoped that he would spend some time with me if I came. I didn't quite imagine, though, that it would be like this."

"Like this?" he inquired.

"Love," I breathed, taking another sip of the wine. "I didn't expect to fall in love."

Claude looked alarmed. "L'amour?" he asked. "Vraiment?" He peered deeply into my eyes, as if my answer really mattered. I couldn't see why he cared so much, but once again I had the nagging thought that there might be another woman in Colman's life. "But aren't you married?"

"Yes," I said.

"And are you going to tear your life up for Colman?"

I shook my head. "No, I am not. Even if I wanted to leave my husband, which I don't, I do not think that we would make a very good married couple. This is just . . ." I searched for the right word. "Magique" is what I came up with. That seemed right. "A moment of pure magic," I repeated. "I am grateful for it. But I know it would not last."

He nodded. "I have found," he said, "that in marriage friendship is sometimes more important than passion."

"Yes," I said. "And my husband is a very good friend."

Claude looked relieved. He liked me well enough, I could see that. He liked the fact that I spoke French. He liked my appetite. But he did not think that I would suit as Colman's wife.

Colman returned, and Claude nodded reassuringly at him. Colman looked relieved, and I felt as if something important had just taken place but I did not know what it was. But then Colman took my hand and the moment passed and we had framboises with Chantilly and cognac and the two men filled the air with the smoke from their cigars. It was dark by the time we left the restaurant, and we put Claude into a taxi and walked all the way back to Colman's hotel, singing.

I was supposed to take the night train back to London, but Colman persuaded me to take the new fast hovercraft across the Channel and spend another day in Paris. When I wavered he just went and bought the ticket. And so we had one more day. And then it really was time for me to leave; I could hardly imagine a life without him anymore. "Stay," he said, laying a bunch of roses on the pillow next to me. "You could take a plane tomorrow and we could still have another day in Paris."

I shook my head. "I'm already gone. It has to end sometime."

"Okay," he said. "I'll take you to the train. We have time for coffee."

"Vous partez?" said our wonderful waitress at Ladurée. "C'est triste. I am so in the habit of seeing you two lovers." And she brought us each a hazelnut-filled croissant and would not let us pay. I bit into it, trying to memorize the taste. "A week from today

I'll be sitting at the kitchen table in Berkeley," I mused, "eating a bowl of millet. And you, what will you be doing a week from this moment?"

Colman reached across the table and took my hand. "I guess the time has come," he said, taking a deep breath. "I don't quite know how to tell you this. But . . ."

"What?" I asked. He looked so stricken that I tried to make things easier. "Don't worry," I said. "We can still see each other. It just won't be the same."

He took another breath, as if to say something, and then stopped. He took my hand and said sadly, "No, it will never be the same again."

Beaujolais Nouveau

Mary Schattenberg

My boyfriend, Steve, and I had been living in our sublet in Paris's fifteenth arrondissement for only about six weeks, and every day we were reminded how little we really knew about our adopted home. Whenever I bought something, I found myself sheepishly watching the cashier place the change carefully on the counter, pointedly avoiding my outstretched hand. At our local cafés, we had yet to arrive during an acceptable mealtime. Every time we ordered food, everyone else was just drinking coffee. And the biggest surprise, just after we arrived, was when the ancient-sounding monthly emergency test siren went off. Deep in a nap, I awoke with a jet-lagged, disoriented start, the completely irrational thought looping through my mind: "The Nazis are coming!"

Late one autumn morning, leaving Steve sleeping, I slipped out the door of our apartment to run along the Seine. Although Paris is the city that invented the public urinal, it does not count exercise among its public activities. So, feeling a bit self-conscious, I carefully made my way along the narrow sidewalks, skirting jovial clusters of pedestrians until I reached the broad boulevard that runs along the river.

There, I hit my stride and let my mind wander. I noticed that, in a nod to the coming millennium, the base of the usually dark Eiffel Tower had been transformed into a giant digital counter. That day was 771. Two years later, we would return to Paris for our honeymoon and witness the other Eiffel Tower change: On the stroke of midnight, 2000, the tower suddenly evaporated into a million glittery sparkles, like a photo shoot, for many minutes. That show was so well received that city officials continued the practice of making the tower sparkle for a few minutes every hour on the hour in the evenings.

As I returned to the apartment, I noticed that the Parisians on the street seemed particularly friendly, chatting with each other as though they had all the time in the world. We had just celebrated Armistice Day (Veterans Day to us Americans)—was this yet another holiday? I spotted the concierge taking out the garbage in the back courtyard of our apartment and considered asking her what was going on—why were Parisians so . . . so uncharacteristically giddy today?

Concierge, a word that English has borrowed from French, conjures up the image of a kindly, know-it-all insider who can get you into the most popular restaurants or sold-out shows in New York. But here in France, I have found concierges to be suspicious, nosy little trolls who live on the ground floor of apartment buildings with many noisy children, cooking fish or some other malodorous meal that permeates the building. Her job, as far as I can tell, is to oversee the comings and goings in the building (i.e., spy), deliver mail, and not, I decided, to act as social coordinator for foreign guests.

For lunch, Steve and I decided to try a new little salad spot on rue Dombasles, just off Convention, owned by a young couple. It was open only during the day, with a limited salad and panini menu. There were usually only a few people there, along with one of the owners prepping food for take-out.

This day was different. Every table was full, so we had to sit at a little counter against the wall. The loud and boisterous patrons were drinking copiously. I had noticed a big sign above the door: *Le Beaujolais Nouveau est arrivé*—signaling that the first crop of Beaujolais wine had arrived. Not knowing the significance of that proclamation, we assumed it referred to an event that evening. It rapidly became clear, though, that it was happening now, and in this hole in the wall, of all places.

We were embarrassed to be so out of it, facing the wall and waiting for our food—and a small carafe of Beaujolais. The background noise was suddenly synchronized and it dawned on me that the crowd was singing—for Christ's sake!—frat boy–style drinking songs. One man held the glass to his forehead, nose, chin, and lower torso (this last body part accentuated with a bawdy flourish), and then everyone sang the French equivalent of "Drink, motherfucker." The person selected by the crowd had to down the entire glass of red wine.

An ambassador for the group, a woman in a leopard-print dress who was reminiscent of Patsy from the BBC-TV show *Absolutely Fabulous*, teetered over to us to explain what was going on. gamely struggling to speak in English, she told us that they were celebrating the official end of the wine season. The goal, she said, was to be the first to taste this year's crop and decide how it compared to those of prior years. She took a shine to Steve, and a few minutes later the whole café was singing to him and making him drink. Steve complied with gusto. They quickly lost interest in him and began grabbing little old men off the street, dragging them inside and giving them glasses of wine.

By and by, we learned more about this festival, which had begun long ago in the villages of Lyons and Beaujolais. Originally an end-of-season reward for vineyard workers, the wine is rushed through production in under a month's time. Whole bunches of gamay grapes are fermented in cooled vats while still in the skin, and pressed within three days. This creates a light, fruity taste with few tannins, a red wine bordering on white that is made to be chilled and gulped, not sipped. It was clear that not much had changed since the first Beaujolais Nouveau festival.

Waving goodbye to the restaurant owners and our new friends, we turned our attention to the single "to do" item on our agenda that day: booking a trip to Prague. We were tipsy enough to realize that a French-only phone conversation was going to be too difficult for a significant financial transaction, so we decided to go directly to the train station to buy the tickets. Waving our bus passes at the driver, we jumped on a bus to Gare de l'Est.

Rosy-cheeked and jocular, we made our way into the depot, and damned if they weren't giving out Beaujolais in the middle of the train station. A giant wagon with a huge wine cask had been rolled in, and women passed it out to all comers. People happily whiled away their time in line, drinking and smoking, for once unconcerned about reaching the agent's window.

Tickets in hand, we headed to the nearest café at five o'clock, our pastis hour. We lingered there and tried to recall which restaurants were advertising special Beaujolais Nouveau dinners. We remembered Chez Clovis, in Les Halles. Walking out of the Metro station, we came upon the most amazing scene—around sixty men, all dressed up in greatcoats, white lacy shirts, and riding boots, playing great round brass hunting horns with all their lung power.

We walked up to a brasserie at the epicenter of the event, and again, everyone was exuberantly and unapologetically drunk. We ordered a plate of smoked meats, *cornichons*, and bread at the bar, then proceeded to the outside "bar" (a flimsy, makeshift counter fashioned out of a pallet and a great slab of cardboard) to watch the men play.

Under a crisp and starry sky, they stood shoulder to shoulder in a kind of marching-band formation that took up the entire street for the length of a block. Young and old listened happily to traditional songs like "La Marseillaise" and standard crowd pleasers like "La Bamba" and "Guantanamera." Cars turning into the middle of the block would find themselves trapped in the crowd. Instead of honking or gesturing angrily, drivers rolled down their windows, and someone promptly gave them a glass of wine to enjoy as they waited to be let through. It was chilly, but the men, most of them in their fifties or sixties, swayed and played in their period outfits for at least two hours, blowing their hearts out.

While some may say that Beaujolais Nouveau is not a "serious" wine, those unfortunate people are missing the point. The race to the table to have a swig of the first pitcher—the uninhibited, joyful spectacle itself—is the point, and thankfully it continues and surprises unsuspecting newcomers to France like us every year.

The Pleasures of the Table

Camille Cusumano

By the time I was no longer interested in having sex with Jean-Pierre, we had made love five times—by a trout stream in the woods near Moustiers Saint-Marie; in three hotels in the south of France; and in his apartment in Aix while his wife was at their villa. For several months now, Jean-Pierre had no longer harbored any hope of my sharing the pleasures of the bed with him. And so the pleasures of the table became our in flagrante delicto, the mutual passion we might be caught at in various places around France.

"*Qu'est-ce qu'il y a?*" Jean-Pierre asked one afternoon as he drove me back to my apartment.

What's wrong? My peevish mind mimicked. Always asking me what's wrong. Always pursing his lips, always the singsong questions. Jean-Pierre was a heavy and nervous smoker. That didn't bother me.

But the birdlike glancing from me to the road, from the road to me, magnified my annoyance. My heart was hard. I knew this.

"*Rien,*" I asserted, letting my throat remain slack and lazy American as I pronounced the word. Nothing was wrong. I looked out my window at the city of Aix, closed up, as always on a Sunday, tight as a fist.

Well, everything was wrong. But it was easier to brood.

Five months earlier I couldn't wait to leave San Francisco. I was at the end of a relationship, in which he-loved-me and I-loved-someone-else. And someone-else was wisely reluctant to complete the triangle. My department chair approved graduate coursework in French in Aix-en-Provence, where I would study art, architecture, and philosophy at l'Université d'Aix-Marseille. My out, I thought. But grief and guilt followed me like the stench of an overripe brie.

On top of my inner gloom, I discovered this: Aix is miserable in winter. No wonder Gertrude Stein, who kept a villa in Provence with Alice B. Toklas, returned to Paris for fall and winter. In winter the Midi is cold and gray as death, clammy as a dying man's hand. And *le mistral!* Too poetic a name for such a brutal, stinging wind. When the wind named for Frédéric M. blew, I found my clothes pathetically thin.

Enter Jean-Pierre, the warmest Frenchman I had yet encountered. I had met him during Mardi Gras weekend. On a whim, I had stood on the autoroute, timidly stuck out my thumb, and gotten a ride from several friendly strangers all the way to Nice for the weekend fanfare. Alone in Nice, I decided I could afford to sleep or eat, but not both. I chose the latter—or perhaps the latter chose me, as the dining hour preceded the sleeping hour. I found myself seated in a nice one-star restaurant, where I ordered the *prix fixe* menu. I sat with Voltaire's *Candide*, propped open so I could eat and read about the absurdity of optimism.

Before my order arrived, a tall blond woman approached my table, speaking halting French. Louise, a Swedish student from my program, had recognized me from our philosophy class. We switched to English, which she spoke perfectly.

"You are so studious," she laughed, "to bring along homework."

"I never expected to meet a soul I knew here," I said.

"Come sit at our table," she said. There I recognized Gunhilde, another Swedish student, and was introduced to Jean-Pierre, who had picked them up, as they were also hitchhiking. Jean-Pierre was a tall, handsome *Normand*, with fine sandy hair, piercing blue eyes, and sharp, classic features. He and Louise looked perfect together, but it was my gaze he held all evening. Certainly my French was better than that of Gunhilde or Louise, but they were the *ravissantes* blonds.

Perhaps Jean-Pierre saw my lust. Not for him—for the rosé, the baguette, *les asperges sauce mousseline*, the little dab of truffle butter on my *daurade* fish. I watched as Jean-Pierre deftly deboned my fish for me, not wasting a smidgen of the coveted flesh. He caught my eyes once and I looked away. When he was done he said, "*Et voilà.*"

I picked up my knife, pushed a morsel of *daurade* onto my fork, and savored it. The room stood still for both of us.

Jean-Pierre had seldom seen such *joie de manger*. As he ordered another bottle of Côtes du Rhone for me, he gently mimicked my immature French "r." Try as he may, he could not say *du rosé* with his lips, anymore than I could trill my r's. He laughed his sandpaper laugh, that night and many nights after.

As I worked carefully on my *tarte aux pommes* so as not to lose a crumb, Louise, Gunhilde, and Jean-Pierre said they had a hotel room I could crash in. Jean-Pierre paid the bill and we left. Before turning in, we strolled alongside Nice's grand parade of huge Disneyland characters on colorful, brightly lit floats. Fireworks showered the sky, and Jean-Pierre grabbed my hand and held it. I let him. We both laughed too hard at *Meecky* and *Meenie* Mouse. Nothing happened that night, but even the Swedes could not help but notice a *coup de foudre*—the proverbial thunderbolt—amid the night's pyrotechnics.

On Sunday morning, Jean-Pierre drove us all home to Aix. He dropped me off last, on rue Roux Alphéron, where I lived in the home of Madame Bulin. I had a fifth floor "garrote," as I called it, that cost $45 a month, the best that I could afford on my stringent budget.

The next day, Jean-Pierre sent me a beautiful handwritten confession explaining that he was married; he asked me to please forgive him for not telling me. He was ashamed of *cette omission*. That evening he showed up at my door with a box of *calissons d'Aix*, the marzipan specialty. I invited him up, and we drank tea in the sitting room with Madame Bulin, her gloved hands hovering around the old knit tea cozy on her teapot. She was an Old World tightwad and would rather wear a drab shawl and shredded gloves than turn on some heat. (She frowned on my American "obsession" with a shower a day—once every five days was indulgent enough for her.)

"*Qu'est-ce qu'il est gentil,*" she informed me, like a parent conveying approval. She thought the gentleman caller was wonderful. And *not* married.

As it turned out, Jean-Pierre's being married was the best arrangement for both him and me. I enjoyed the physical intimacy at first, which tempered one appetite. And he loved his wife, Nathalie—though, he explained, "*Elle mange que des bricoles.*" She ate little this-and-that's, little snacks. What she devoured was American and English literature—by the yard. And here I was, eager to devour French food with equal fervor. So while Jean-Pierre's wife stayed home most weekend nights to read Iris Murdoch, Joyce Carol Oates, or Norman Mailer, he and I pored over the heavenly aromas and flavors that I had read about. Jean-Pierre spoke of her to me as *ma femme* and of me to Nathalie, I surmised, as *l'étudiante* or *l'Américaine*, though it was not clear to me how much his wife knew about our affair.

"*Elle est toute petite,*" Jean-Pierre described her for me, "*cambrée.*" He moved his hands to help me imagine a "cambered" woman. Shapely, blond, blue-eyed. As introverted as Jean-Pierre was outgoing, she eschewed most socializing. I knew how *toute petite* she was long before I ever met Nathalie. One evening in the apartment with Jean-Pierre—Nathalie was at their villa—I spotted in a corner her size four pumps. They looked like doll shoes. Her little *tartine* toasts, and *crocotte*, crackers, all she ate, were on the counter, partly nibbled.

One night, several months into our regularly scheduled gastronomic gorging, Jean-Pierre introduced me to my first *quenelles,* down the road from Aix on a *café-terrace* in Tholonet. As usual, the days preceding consumption of the meal were filled with detailed conversation about the feast. Jean-Pierre, a scientist by trade, could wax poetic on any kitchen creation. "These delicate airy dumplings," he explained as we salivated in tandem, "are made of ground fish mixed with egg whites, poached in stock, and covered in a shellfish sauce."

I was stretching my lexicon of French culinary terms, but it was small compensation for the classes I was skipping and the intellectual pursuits I was ignoring—things for which I had, after all, come to France.

I had come to Provence with a fail-safe plan—to take refuge from my emotional confusion back home. I had envisioned myself so deeply immersed in Camus, Sartre, Rousseau, and Voltaire that I would hardly notice such transient phenomena as hormones or heartache. I would spend hours in the garishly lit library, so absorbed with some esoteric theme for a future doctoral dissertation that I would ignore hunger pangs, even libido, and fade into a gaunt, hollow-cheeked pedagogue. I would follow in the path of Simone de Beauvoir and be one of those rare female contributors to the body of philosophy.

I hated to admit to myself that I felt more like the disenchanted and doomed *personnages* of Flaubert's *Madame Bovary*, Prévost's *Manon Lescaut*, Zola's *Nana*. Furthermore, Jean-Pierre was not Jean-Paul Sartre. He was full of conventions and earthiness and practicalities. Our mealtime talk would not have made for a feature-length film to rival *My Dinner with Andre*. And instead of expounding a thesis, I was expanding my body.

Our laughter filled the night in Tholonet and the fullness from the food and wine temporarily masked other longings. But then, as if I were a Catholic-school girl who had to pick something she enjoyed to give up for Lent, I said, "No more sex."

"*Pourquoi?*" Jean-Pierre asked. I didn't have a satisfactory answer. It would have been dishonest to say that it was because he was married, or that I was not ready to feast on a new love until I had cleared my palate of the previous one—though these tidy excuses did come to mind. Nor was it because sex felt like payment for a meal I could not afford. But somehow, odd as it sounds, perverse as it still seems today, I felt that as long as we were sharing orgasms at the table, it was redundant to indulge in the pleasures of the bed.

Jean-Pierre, of course, saw things otherwise, but after a while he stopped asking *pourquoi* and said, "*C'est triste. Et, oui, c'est triste.*" And yet he continued to show me places in his country I would not have gotten to on my own, always orchestrated to culminate at a fine one- or two-star restaurant. We made trips to Saint-Maximin-La-Sainte-Baume, a cloisters and basilica with a beautiful organ; to Moustiers-Sainte-Marie, where he bought me a lovely piece of French *faïence* with a brilliant blue glaze the color of his eyes. He bought me *santons*, the Provençal clay dolls dressed as peasants in calico. He took me to the Gorge du Verdon, the Grand Canyon of France with its two-thousand-foot-deep narrow-throated canyon.

Before Jean-Pierre, I was happy to subsist on dense, brown, golden-raisin-filled bread. I bought it piping hot every morning at the Boulangerie Madeleine, wrapped in a piece of brown paper. On my way to eat it at Café Madeleine with two cafés au lait, I'd tear into it, steam issuing into the cold morning. In my little room, I kept a jar of *confiture d'abricots* to slather on it sometimes—a dangerous habit, as I'd eat the whole jar of apricot jam when the weather got depressing.

But now, Jean-Pierre educated my palate in the art of French cuisine—revealing how the chefs' alchemy worked on grouse, pheasant, partridge, quail, woodcock, loin of hare, or venison saddle, steeped in a classic reduction sauce, infused with herbs and essences, finished with the delicacy and restraint that the French have perfected.

We went to Marseilles once and climbed way up to Notre Dame de la Garde, the patron saint of sailors. *"Regarde, regarde,"* he pointed excitedly out to sea, at the Chateau d'If from *The Count of Monte Cristo*. Then, down along the harbor, we watched in rapt silence as a waiter waved our caged salmon filet over smoke redolent of burning stalks of fennel, a natural foil for the oily fish.

For the fun of it, we photographed the evidence of our complete consummation—platters piled with fish bones picked clean of flesh: perhaps the gourmand's equivalent of the lover's rumpled bed.

"Do you tell Nathalie about me?" I asked. I began to want to know her, this woman whose husband was becoming a friend of mine.

"*Oui,*" he said.

"Does she want to meet me?"

"*Oui.*"

"When?"

He didn't know when. When he was ready. He wrinkled his brow and looked full of sorrow, and I knew that in those furrows lay the hope that I'd become his lover again. In which case, it would be best if she and I didn't become friends.

He always ended this conversation assuring me, "*Elle n'est pas dupe.*" She's nobody's dupe. But I knew I was not a threat to their marriage any more than she was a threat to our budding friendship. Ironically, I had left one triangle only to find a place in another.

Every weekday evening, I saw Jean-Pierre for two hours after he got off work and before he returned for supper with his wife. He returned by bus from Cadareche, where he worked as a nuclear technician. We rendezvoused at 5:00 P.M. at the bus stop by the fountains at the bottom of the Cour Mirabeau. We strolled the Cour Mirabeau and sat at Deux Garçons, which he hated for its *snobisme,* which I loved it for. He drank, in two slurps, *un espress',* made syrupy with two heaping teaspoons of sugar. Gauloise smoke curled from his Gallic nose and mouth and enveloped us as he explained to me about the chi-chi, bourgeois *Aixois*. I nursed, without exception, a 51 pastis—never Pernod—with *un carafe d'eau*. Jean-Pierre would laugh his grinding laugh at how I said "carafe of water" in French.

And, as I let go of the script I had arrived in France with, I found I had become part of a tableau of no less import, I thought, than the salons of the Left Bank.

Before Jean-Pierre left to sup with Nathalie each evening, he took me shopping in the basement of Prisunic. He bought me my first *rillettes*, *crème fraîche*, *salsify*, and Pont l'Eveque cheese—a whole square of it. I would climb to my garrote with my arms full, look out over the orange clay-top roofs of Aix, and feel alternately uncertain of the relationships I was forging in my host culture and blessed to be amid the timeless countryside of Cézanne's inspiration (this was all long before author Peter Mayle made Provence all too prominent on the tourist circuit).

If I wasn't growing intellectually, I certainly was physically. My clothes got tighter as I filled them to the max. The more I ate, the more I craved. And Jean-Pierre was ever ready to sate all longings with food. One night he returned from Cadareche to find me unusually low. I blamed it on the cold, the abandoned boyfriend, the bourgeois shopkeeper who scolded me for squeezing a tomato.

"Come, let's visit *la pâtisserie* near place du Verdun," he said. He knew I loved *la glace française* and he insisted I order some.

The Pleasures of the Table

"*Ca te fera du bien.*" It will make everything right. "*Alors, viens, mange.*" Three scoops—*noisette, vanille,* and *café,* with chocolate syrup, crunchy meringues, *crème chantilly,* nuts. It always worked. And then spring broke out like an uncontained smile. Provence, like a butterfly breaking out of its chrysalis, cycled into olive, fruit, and almond trees in pink and white bud. The plane trees along the Cour Mirabeau billowed into their fabled tunnel of foliage. Cézanne's Mont Sainte-Victoire rose boldly, its bauxite folds a silver beacon against the neon-bright sky. Everywhere, one inhaled rosemary, thyme, lavender, garlic—all in the same breath. It was hard to remain depressed.

But I still retained a touch of *mal au coeur*—I loved the French for having a tag line for my garden-variety heartsickness. On this day in April, Jean-Pierre was taking me to his native village in Normandy to eat *choucroute*—my first *choucroute*—with his family for Easter Sunday. The Norman countryside was lush with dairy farms and thatched-roof Tudor houses. We stayed one night in a small village and had lake trout and, of course, *du rosé* at Au Faisan Doré.

We spent Holy Saturday at Jean-Pierre's sister Dominique's flat in Deauville, sleeping on the living room floor. Dominique was thrilled to meet me. No one even mentioned Nathalie. That evening, Jean-Pierre grabbed my housecoat and tried it on. It was comically too small for him—it fit him like a jacket. He postured and walked around the room like a bent dowager. Dominique laughed. Her boyfriend, Michel, laughed, too.

I didn't laugh. I was annoyed for a trivial reason—the scent of his French cologne was on my robe—and made the mistake of expressing it. Dominique and Michel went to bed. Jean-Pierre, who had spared nothing in trying to improve my mood, sat quietly on the floor where we were to sleep on blankets. His voice was harsh, the way it was when he railed at his fellow drivers, whom he wanted to assassinate for being imbeciles.

"*C'est incroyable!*" his voice scratched, "*toi alors!*" I couldn't understand all the heated French pouring out of him, only *égoïste*—selfish—and *Qu'est-ce que je peux, moi? Rien, rien! J'y peux rien! Rien du tout!* What can I do? *Rien*, he answered himself, over and over. And just as these "nothing"s reached critical mass, he did something I had never seen him do. Jean-Pierre began to sob. And sob. His whole body heaved and writhed. He sobbed so hard that my blues suddenly assumed a smallness that hadn't seemed possible. I realized that since the time we had moved our relationship out of the bedroom, he had accumulated a lot of grief. He was giving vent to it now.

"*Je suis désolée, Jean-Pierre,*" I said. But the words felt like *rien*, nothing. His tears were far too formidable to warrant discussion. We went to sleep, and slept deeply.

The next morning, Jean-Pierre was up before me, laughing his raucous laugh with Dominique and Michel. I walked to the beach and passed Deauville's big, silent casino. I watched the brown Atlantic rollers along yellow sandy beaches, the weathered shore houses. They reminded me of the Jersey shore in fall after the summer masses left—one of the things I missed about the East Coast, where I had grown up. I skipped a stone over the back of a wave and ran back to the apartment.

Jean-Pierre was cheerful as we drove, and I shared his enthusiasm. It was Easter Sunday, and I was going to taste this Alsatian specialty—*choucroute*—made with a variety of sausages and fermented cabbage. Best of all, I was going to be welcomed into the home of French people who had made their life on this land for many generations, who had bittersweet memories of *les Américains* coming to liberate France. And, I was achieving what every American told me was impossible—friendship with a Frenchman.

We drove far into a countryside of passionately green rolling pastures, the morning mist rising like amiable specters from the wet ground. At Jean-Pierre's family's home, we drank beer, and then Muscadet and Sancerre with the *choucroute*. At first I was surprised when a mundane platter of sauerkraut and sausages was set before me. But no, this dish was more complex than it looked, saturated with the sweet pungency of fermented cabbage, slightly caramelized, and the robust flavors of grain-fed meats. It was certainly not mundane.

No one seemed curious about where Jean-Pierre's wife was. Everyone treated me like a special guest. I was surprised by his mother's weathered body and coarse appearance, but not by the effusive affection that flowed between Jean-Pierre and her. After the main course, we walked, three generations deep, down the village street to a meadow. Jean-Pierre showed me where to pick handfuls of streamside *cresson*, the watercress for the next course, which we would eat after we had had time to digest the first. There, in the soil fed by constant fresh water, an edible green flourished.

In a strange parallel, Jean-Pierre's tears had purged and watered some hidden riparian corridor. I didn't know at that moment that our friendship would flourish over the next two decades as we made trips to each other's countries. Nor that I would soon meet Nathalie and that we would become good friends and write each other often—she in English, I in French—and that she would one day present me with a family heirloom, a silver platter. One day, after some twenty-five years of marriage, Jean-Pierre would temporarily leave Nathalie for another woman (did she love to eat, too? I never asked). He would still visit Nathalie every day. Nathalie would be brokenhearted, but not for long. For he would return to her.

At last, in the midst of Jean-Pierre's earthy family, I felt some inner peace. As we gathered the leafy bunches from his succulent countryside to bring back to the table, and the sound of provincial French bubbled around us, I told him I was happy to be there. This small gratitude, genuinely expressed, was as nourishing to us as a stream to wild greens.

Many years later, I found a bittersweet commentary on my and Jean-Pierre's—and Nathalie's—story in the words of an eighteenth-century Frenchman, Jean-Anthelme Brillat-Savarin: "The pleasures of the table . . . go hand in hand with all our other pleasures, outlast them, and remain to console us for their loss."

My French Fetish

Lisa Solod

I am sitting in an exclusive shop on the Champs Elysées trying on boots. The boots have the highest heels I have ever seen—at least four inches. They are the height of *le look*—an ironic borrowing from English for something that is quintessentially French.

As I struggle to zip the boots up over my calves, the salesclerk rushes to my aid. She pushes my flesh down, like sausage into its casing. My natural reflex is to suck everything in, so I hold my breath while the waif takes the zipper from my hands and tugs it firmly up, up, up.

French women, if you have not noticed, are not only smaller around the hips, waist, and bust, but also have smaller feet and legs than American women. Buying a size eight shoe at home in the United States puts me in an anonymous average category. In France, a special franchise is required for women of my shoe size (although it is worth noting that many French women routinely wear a size smaller than they need).

My calves feel fat, thick, and corseted, and I am breathless, as though I were wearing a tight brassiere. I feel faint. I stand up and wobble to and fro. The clerk catches me just before I go over, fluttering my arms like butterfly wings—though nothing that dainty could describe my appearance.

Embarrassed, I explain it's my ankles—not the boots. *"Vous voyez,* my ankles—they were always weak . . . I was never much of an ice skater . . . they were barely able to hold me,"* I babble in my best Franglais.

"Jolies! Elles vous vont bien," she says, ignoring the problem of my equilibrium.

The boots put so much distance between me and the ground, they feel like stilts. But even worse than the vertigo and the sense that I look like some bizarre circus performer, I suddenly see myself as a six-year-old clacking around the house in my mother's high heels.

The salesgirl eyes me critically. If she is amused, she hides it well. "Perhaps you would like to try something that is less high?" she suggests in accented English that is so professional in tone, I feel like making a joke. But before I can poke fun at myself, she adds, "These are, after all, the highest we have." With that, I detect the slightest twinkle in her eye—and I know I'll be fodder for her dinner conversation: *"Alors,* I had another one of those American girls—you know, with calves the size of my waist."

"Oh, no," I say, taking a deep breath and dismissing her sugges-
tion with every ounce of my lovely and curvy figure. "I want to try
these." I have no intention of buying the boots. But walking in them
has become a matter of pride. I'm also curious how it will feel.

"I'll just step over here off the carpet, OK?" I say, ignoring her
worried look. The salesgirl nods her consent.

I stand and look at myself in the full-length mirror and try not to
laugh. I look absolutely ridiculous. The boots are a mile long and a
mile high, and I cannot even take a step without fear of falling and
breaking a bone. The posture is so alien to my sense of sexuality that
I see myself as a man dressed up as a woman, a hooker, a closet cross-
dresser, a *je ne sais quoi*. But this self-humiliation was something I had
to do. For weeks I have been listening to the clack-clack-clack of high
heels on the sidewalk. Even with my shutters tightly closed and the
drapes and sheers drawn, the street noises filter up to my third-floor
window in the most chic of arrondissements, the sixteenth, where
women routinely look as though they have just stepped out of the
pages of *Vogue*. I also hear voices and dogs, cars, and motorcycles,
lovers arguing and children crying. Yet the sound that has trumped
all, the little rat-tat sound that drowns out all the others, is that of
heels clattering along the pavement.

Je l'adore!

I have always been obsessed with heels. And now, months into
my first year in Paris, my eyes barely travel above ankle level—taking
in the delicately elevated sandals, the backless slides, the pumps, the
boots. I have a fetish for shoes. I have watched French women in

three-and-a-half-inch spike heels push baby carriages, lug groceries home from the Monoprix. Women in slides dainty as slippers or mules with toes sleek as knife blades and heels sharp as daggers run for the subway and over the grates in the streets, slip into cars with standard shifts, or march along the sandy soil of the Bois de Boulogne. *Les femmes françaises* maneuver the steps of Montmartre in shoes that would have me begging to be put out of my misery.

And despite this torture, French women have very beautiful, very well-cared-for feet. Their toenails, uniformly and gorgeously polished, peek out of thinly strapped sandals, especially in August and September. Their heels are smooth as glass, and there is nary a corn or bunion in sight. Podiatrist-pedicurists line the streets of all the best neighborhoods, many offering the standard pedicure at prices no higher than those in my small town in Virginia. It's as if feet were poodles to be groomed—and so they are: pets of a sort.

Blindsided by shoe envy and my fixation with feet, I vowed to visit at least one of these pet salons for *le pied* before I donned sandals in the spring. I had pedicures each month during the spring and summer, at half a dozen salons, before I found the perfect fit. As I expected, those doctors of the foot were miracle workers. How else to explain the beauty of a foot elevated on a three-inch heel, traipsing down a filthy, dog-feces-ridden sidewalk and over broken concrete and cobblestones, a foot that, against all odds, remains fetching and unscathed?

The heeled footwear of the Parisian is anorexic compared with the shoes I wore as a young career woman in the United States. This is part of the allure for an avowed shoe slut. I salivate over the very smell of their leather, the way French chefs drool over dirt-caked truffles or a bloody mound of calf's liver. I adore beautiful shoes, shoes that make the legs look long and sexy, shoes that cant the body slightly forward, shoes that make a woman, no matter how much a feminist, look ever so helpless and vulnerable. My addiction trumps political correctness.

Until today, I have only bought shoes with heels of a height that permits one to walk down the street in comfort and safety, without looking like a fool. And yet, after the third—or fourth—time passing a particular store on the Champs Elysées, I could no longer resist knowing those high heels, intimately. As if trying to outdo one another in this phenomenally French obsession, Parisian shoe stores feature immense diversity—style, color, shape, and form vary greatly from boutique to boutique. I had to slip on one pair of the highest heels and experience them, to see for myself what is possible, or even plausible.

I had to know firsthand my place among women who, no matter their age or mobility—dowagers, teenagers, middle-aged housewives, even those who walk assisted—wear the world's highest heels. I had witnessed women of a certain age outfitted in the most stylish of shoes, their flesh spilling over the edges, while their caregivers literally held them up as the two tramped down the street in unsuitable shoes. As often, I had seen mothers with infants running, in stilettos, for the bus. It was too much to bear. And what, too, of the stress to the lumbar region? Well, it's another French paradox, akin to the one where their butterfat-rich diet correlates with squeaky-clean arteries. French women walk tall—and they do so, it seems, with impunity.

I stood tall in that stunning pair of black leather boots, their pointy toes reaching a good three inches beyond my own cramped and calloused ones, their heels making me as tall as I thought I should be—even if my trim and muscular calves, which I had been previously quite fond of, bulged out over the tops of the zippers.

Perhaps it is as Edith Wharton explains in her little-read *French Ways and Their Meanings*: The French, in general, prefer occasional splendor to everyday comfort, a preference that most American women cannot fathom. For Parisians the street is a stage and the show must go on, no matter the weather or the measure of discomfort. When one steps from one's apartment and out onto the sidewalk, the responsibility begins: The costume must be appropriate. The beauty of the city of Paris itself is overwhelming, and those who enter that setting pay homage to it with their appearance.

But in the end, I reluctantly peel the boots off my swollen and aching feet and admit that I cannot participate in this particular mise en scène. I shall have to feel chic in my slightly more low-heeled *chaussures*. I hand the boots back to the saleswoman and shake my head ruefully, with a tinge of real regret.

"No," I tell her, with enough warmth in my voice to let her know I have given the matter careful thought. "*Merci beaucoup, madame.*"

She looks bewildered, as if she wants to object to the assertion I have not made that it is not possible to walk in shoes like these. But she does not explain what I soon come to understand.

Days later, I overhear this conversation in Charles Jourdan:

Customer: Aren't these awfully high?

Saleswoman: Oh, yes, they are for dress only—they are *sitting* shoes.

Customer: Oh, yes, of course.

Sitting shoes? If only I had known.

The Dirt on French Service

Rikke Jorgensen

"There's a pubic hair in my pasta," I said calmly, with as much dignity as I could muster. Across the table from me, Karen paused in mid-chew and put down her utensils, her eyes quickly scanning the surrounding diners for any undue attention. Perhaps they'd heard me say "pubic." We were in Grenoble, where people understood English very well. She carefully moved the silver pot of flowering lavender out of the way, leaned over the white-draped table, and inspected the curly black hair, complete with white bulbous follicle, sitting on a freshly made goat cheese and spinach ravioli like an innocent bit of extra garnish.

"Could be a chest hair," she said.

Karen is English and will suffer almost any humiliation quietly rather than make a fuss.

"It's too curly for a chest hair. Could be from an armpit, I will give you that," I said, raising a hand to get the waiter's attention. "Pit or crotch, I'm not going to eat it."

"You could just put it to one side," Karen suggested. The fingers of her right hand smoothed the napkin against the table. "I mean, what are you hoping to achieve?"

English or not, in this instance Karen wasn't merely adhering to a genetic and cultural disposition for confrontation avoidance. Having lived in Grenoble for years, she had reason to question what greater good complaining would serve. In a comparable situation in England or the United States, apologies would have been forthcoming, as would a fresh portion or a different dish at no charge. But this was France, and we both knew better.

Only three days earlier, on a cobblestone square in Aix-en-Provence, I had been served a salad with lollo rossa lettuce, artichoke hearts, pine nuts, and dirt. Not a modest little dusting of dirt crunching between my teeth, revealing a somewhat superficial rinsing, but a hearty clump of good French soil. I could have grown cress in it. I showed the waitress, a wired, thirtyish woman, expecting a modicum of remorse and a new salad. Instead I got an overbearing smile and the words "C'est un peu de terre . . ."

It's a bit of dirt. What's all the to-do about? When I insisted that the dirt should not be in my salad, she looked at me as if I were a Chihuahua having a yapping fit, tore off the ruffled lettuce leaf where the clump resided, and threw it on the ground in front of my sandaled feet. "Voilà!" Then she walked off to serve her less demanding customers.

I generally prefer my salads without compost, and any type of hair in my food will dramatically reduce the chances of repeat business from me for the establishment in question. But I appreciate the lack of humility displayed by the average French service provider. Though occasionally counterproductive in terms of business, it is at the very least honest. At best, it is what France is all about: a sense of equality and pride, a refusal to ingratiate. Compare this with the American cashier squeezing out "Thank you for shopping at Wal-Mart" when all he really wants is for you to pick up your change and exit his personal planet. American service is second to none when it comes to free water expediently delivered at the table, Disney smiles, and verbal smoothies, but the pleasantries are often so forced and artificial they leave you feeling more resented than by the irreverent French.

Service is considered an unnecessary extra in France—a luxury reserved for the staggeringly rich and powerful. Ordinary people should not expect to be pampered; life is not for the cosseted, or the easily deterred. Casual disdain is a part of life. An enthusiastically served meal belongs in Greece or Italy, not France. The liquid mix of charm and superiority that characterizes the hotel receptionist, the boutique owner, the greengrocer, is a language of its own: of sighs, pregnant pauses, slow, feline gestures, and shamelessly verbose eyebrows.

Familiar with this language, I was not expecting heartfelt apologies or faces burning with humiliation at my presentation of the hair, even in the relatively expensive restaurant where Karen and I were dining on the evening in question. Setting myself what I considered to be a realistic goal, I was aiming for a replacement portion, *sans* pubes.

When I managed to attract the attention of our whiskered headwaiter, he floated over and asked with a half-smile what he could do for me. I pointed out the curled-up evidence. He sighed and then looked at me as though he would love to help, and was saddened by the fact that he could not, as if I had just asked him to donate a kidney. He shook his slick, dark head slowly and said, "It is not mine . . ."

Food to which Aunt Pauline and Lady Godiva led us

Alice B. Toklas

When in 1916 Gertrude Stein commenced driving Aunt Pauline for the American Fund for French Wounded, she was a responsible if not an experienced driver. She knew how to do everything but go in reverse. She said she would be like the French Army, never have to do such a thing. Delivering to hospitals in Paris and the suburbs offered no difficulties, for there was practically no civilian traffic. One day we were asked to make a delivery to a military hospital in Montereau, where we would lunch after the visit to the hospital. It was late by the time that had been accomplished and the court of the inn that had been recommended was crowded with military cars. When Gertrude Stein proposed leaving Aunt Pauline, for so our delivery truck had been baptised—not in champagne, only in white wine—in the entrance of the court, I protested. It was barring the exit. We can't leave it in the road, she said. That would be too tempting. The large dining-room was filled with officers. The lunch, for wartime, was good. We were waiting for coffee when an officer came to our table and, saluting, said, The truck with a Red Cross in the entrance to the court belongs to you. Oh yes, we proudly said in unison. It is unfortunately barring the exit, he said, so that none of the cars in the court can get out. I am afraid I must ask you to back it out. Oh that, cried Gertrude Stein, I can not do, as if it were an unpardonable sin he were asking her to commit. Perhaps, he continued, if you come with me we might together be able to do it. Which they did. But Gertrude Stein was not yet convinced that she would have to learn to go in reverse.

If Aunt Pauline had led us to Montereau on her first adventure, she was soon doing better. The committee of the American Fund had asked us to open a depot for distributing to several departments with headquarters at Perpignan. Aunt Pauline—Model T, bless her— made no more than thirty miles an hour, so we were always late at inns, hotels and restaurants for meals. But at Saulieu they would serve us for lunch *Panade Veloutée*, Ham Croquettes and *Peches Flambées*. They were cooked with delicacy and distinction.

As we came into the dining-room I had noticed a man wandering about whose appearance disturbed me, he looked suspiciously like a German. German officer prisoners did occasionally escape. When the *maître d'hôtel* received our compliments for the fine cooking, I asked him who the man was and he said he was the proprietor of the hotel and had just been released from Germany where he had been a civilian prisoner. He had been *chef* for a number of years to the Kaiser, which not only accounted for the quality of the food but for the clothes which had misled me.

Aunt Pauline took several days to get us to Lyon where we were to lunch at La Mère Fillioux's famous restaurant. As a centre of gastronomy it was famous for a number of dishes, so La Mère Fillioux's menu was typical of Lyon. It was the habit in Lyon and thereabouts for restaurants and hotels to have set menus called *le diner fin* and *le déjeuner fin*, the choicest dinner and the choicest lunch. We had her choicest lunch, *Lavarets au beurre,** hearts of artichokes with truffled foie gras, steamed capon with *quenelles* and a *tarte Louise*. Lyon is an excellent marketing centre. Fish served at lunch is caught in the morning, vegetables and fruits are of that morning's picking, which is of first importance in their preparation. Mère Fillioux was a short compact woman in a starched enveloping apron with a short, narrow but formidable knife which she brandished as she moved from table to table carving each chicken. That was her pleasure and her privilege which she never relinquished to another. She was an expert carver. She placed a fork in the chicken once and for all. Neither she nor the plate moved, the legs and the wings fell, the two breasts, in less than a matter of minutes, and she was gone. After the war, she carved a fair-sized turkey for eight of us with the same technique and with as little effort. When the fish appeared at our table she came to it and passed her hand about an inch above

Note: Lavarets are fish found in the lakes of Switzerland and the *Haute Savoie*.

our plates to see that they were of the right temperature. Later she returned and with her little knife carved the largest and whitest chicken I ever saw. A whole chicken was always dedicated to each table, even if there was only one person at it. Not to have any small economies gave style to the restaurant. What remained of the chicken no doubt became the base of the forcemeat for the *quenelles* that were made freshly each morning.

Aunt Pauline eventually got us to Perpignan where we settled down to work. At the quiet hotel we had selected there was a banquet hall, closed for the duration of the war. I made arrangements to use it as a depot from which to distribute, the greater part to serve as a warehouse for the material already awaiting us at the station, and a corner to be screened off to serve us as an office where we could receive doctors and nurses who would come with lists of their individual needs. The hotel was delightful. There were wartime restrictions, and a few privations, but each guest was hoveringly cared for by one or more members of a family of four. The cooking was excellent, southern—not Provençal but Catalan. The Rousillon had been French for little more than 150 years.

There had been difficulty in getting gasoline on the coupons the army gave us. The major who was in charge of this distribution had been very helpful. Gertrude Stein did not like going to offices—she said they, army or civilian, were obnoxious. To replace her, I had introduced myself with her official papers and had allowed the major to call me Miss Stein. What difference could it make to him. We were just two Americans working for French wounded. By the time the difficulties had been overcome we had become quite friendly. At the last visit he said, Miss Stein, my wife and I want to know if you both want to dine with us some evening. It was time to acknowledge who I was. He drew back in his chair and with a violence that alarmed me said, Madame, there is something sinister in this affair. My explanation did not completely reassure him, but Gertrude Stein waiting in Aunt Pauline in the street below would. I asked him if he wouldn't go down with me to meet her. He did. Her cheerful innocence was convincing, and his invitation was repeated and accepted. They were delightful. Madame de B. was training a local cook to cook as she believed cooking should be done.

During wars, no game is allowed to be shot in France except boar that come down into the fields and do great damage. To prevent this a permit is given to landowners to shoot them on their property. A farmer had shot one and brought the saddle to Madame de B. So we had roasted saddle of young boar.

We had visited all the hospitals in the region and had reported on their future needs. Having made our last distributions we closed the depot at Perpignan and returned to Paris for another assignment. By this time, 1917, the United States had broken relations with

Germany and had declared war. At last we were no longer neutral. On the road to Nevers, as Gertrude Stein was changing spark plugs— and when was one not in those days—we were told that a detachment of Marines was expected there that afternoon. Aunt Pauline was pushed to her utmost speed that we might be there for the entry. Thrilled by the first sight of the doughboys, we were unprepared for their youth, vigour and gaiety compared to the fatigue and exhaustion of the French soldiers. We were asked by some of their officers to meet the soldiers that evening and tell them about France. They had dozens of questions to ask, but what they wanted most to know was how many miles they were from the front and why the French trucks made such a noise. Though they were disappointed in our answers we had a wonderful and exciting evening together. It was their first contact with France and ours with our army.

In Paris the A.F.F.W. proposed we should open a depot at Nîmes where in advance of our arrival they would send several car-loads of material. News of our household was not so encouraging. During our absence our competent faithful Jeanne had gotten herself married. An excellent cook who worked by the hour consented to spend with us the few days we were to be in Paris. Severe rationing of meat, butter, eggs, gas and electricity had gone into effect. A small reserve of coal and assorted candles gave meagre heat and light. Ernestine accomplished much with little which permitted us to ask for lunch some of the Field Service men and volunteer nurses on leave in Paris.

❖

The luxury hotel at Nîmes was in a sad way. The proprietor had been killed at the war, the *chef* was mobilised, the food was poor and monotonous. Aunt Pauline had been militarised and so could be requisitioned for any use connected with the wounded. Gertrude Stein evacuated the wounded who came into Nîmes on the ambulance trains. Material from our unit organised and supplied a small first-aid operating room. The Red Cross nuns in the best French manner served in large bowls to the wounded piping hot chocolate.

Monsieur le Préfet and his wife, *Madame la Préfete*, whom we got to know and to like a lot, sent us word that a regiment of American soldiers was expected, that a camp was being prepared for them and that he would like us to be at the station with him when they arrived. Nîmes was agog with excitement and welcomed them as best it could—green wreaths, bunting and flags. Thanksgiving Day was some ten days after the soldiers arrived. Even the most modest homes were inviting our soldiers to lunch or to dinner to celebrate the day. That evening we had for dinner a large tableful of soldiers from camp. The manageress of the hotel, a large buxom blonde, had a group of American officers at her table. They were perhaps too noticeably gay.

At dinner one night—the inevitable whiting with its tail in its mouth was our monotonous fare—what appeared undoubtedly to be a German passed our table. This is really going too far, I said to Gertrude Stein. How dare an escaped prisoner show himself so publicly, so brazenly. Not your affair, let the authorities deal with him, she answered. After dinner the too-gay manageress said to me, There is a gentleman who has been asking to speak to you. I will send for him. It was the German. In perfect English he said he wished to speak to us alone a moment, and he pointed to some chairs. Gertrude Stein, always cheerful, agreeable and curious, sat down but not I. Who are you and what do you want of us, I asked. I do want some information from you, but first let me introduce myself. I am Samuel Barlow and we have several friends in common, but I am here as an officer in the secret service, in civvies naturally, to find out what is going on between yonder gay blonde and the American officers. The *Préfet* reported the case to us. He says he has reason to believe she is a German. Well, said I relieved, rather she than you. I mistook you for a German. My only civilian clothes, he said, were from Germany where I was a prisoner. This ended my concern with escaping German prisoners.

At Christmas the English wife of a prominent Nîmois organised, with the aid of the English companions and governesses who had posts in Nîmes, a dinner and dance for the British convalescent officers and men stationed there, and requisitioning for their army at Arles. After dinner we took turns dancing with the men. It was as gay as we could make it but the British Army was not cheerful. A few days later I had a visit from the prettiest of the young governesses. She said there had been an unfortunate incident after the party was over. She was preparing to turn out the light in her bedroom when there was a tap on the door which evidently connected with another room, and a voice asked, I say, Miss L., should I light my fire. Too surprised to answer, she was silent for a moment. The question was repeated, I say, Miss L., should I light my fire. Not for me, thank you, she answered. Of course the voice was unrecognisable, she ended, so I will never know which one of them it was.

Suddenly one day there was the Armistice and a telegram from the *Comité*—If you speak German, close the depot immediately, return to proceed Alsace civilian relief. If we had missed the spontaneous outburst of joy in Paris on Armistice Day we were going into liberated Alsace. One starlit morning we started in Auntie to make the six hundred odd kilometres to Paris before night. Gertrude Stein ate her share of bread and butter and roast chicken while driving. Paris was still celebrating, and here the streets were commencing to be filled with the French Army, on the move into occupied Germany, and a certain number of Allied officers and men.

Having secured a German-French dictionary and fur-lined aviator's jackets and gloves, cumbersome but warm, we got off on the road again. The French Army was moving in the same direction Auntie was taking us. Near Tulle the mules dragging the regimental kitchen became unruly, swerved to the left and bumped into Auntie. A mudguard, the tool box and its contents scattered on the road and into the ditch. There was, of course, no way of recovering them. Starting off again, Gertrude Stein found the triangle so damaged as to make driving on the icy road not only difficult but possibly dangerous. We got to Nancy exhausted, too late for dinner, but Dorothy Wilde sweetly found two hard-boiled ducks' eggs, a novel but very satisfying repast. While Auntie was being repaired next day at the garage of the *Comité*, we had our first meal without restrictions.

After which Aunt Pauline took us through no-man's-land to Strasbourg, still celebrating the Liberation. That night there was a torchlight procession of soldiers and civilians, the young girls in their attractive costumes (the black ribbon head-dress they had worn since 1870 changed to all the colours of the rainbow), with military bands. It was more like a dream than a reality. We were now in the land of plenty.

Speaking French

Judy Kronenfeld

When I speak French, a language I studied in high school and college, the words pass before my eyes as though they're moving across a screen. As I round my lips for the vowels or feel my nose tighten for the nasalization, the words glide by on a schoolgirl's mental blackboard, accompanied by their bizarre fantails of mysterious or silent letters—*journAUX, batEAU, fauTEUIL*—though I know to say journO, batO, foeTOY. I once heard that medieval scribes produced justified right margins by adding those endings full of attitude. My husband has never studied the language formally, but has picked up a thimbleful on the street. So, whereas I see *j'aime, tu aimes, ils aiment*, he hears *J'M, Tu M, Ilz M*; it's as if his French is a kind of pig Latin.

The mental blackboard does not disappear when I grow a bit more accustomed to speaking French. Nor does it produce an annoying sensation. On the contrary, it is more than a pleasant one, a constant reaffirmation. Just asking for my bread at *la boulangerie*, buying my wine at *la cave au vin*, I feel I have managed to cross the gated divide between the letters of French words and their actual pronunciation. I ask the severe and proper madame in her white apron—punctiliously waiting on the pressing crowd in the bakery— for *une à l'ancienne*, just ever so slightly prolonging the final nasal. She sings back *"à l'ancienne-nuh,"* without blinking an eye, and emphasizes her own final syllable just a pinch more (in that way the French have of making even the most mundane exchange into a language lesson). I know I have passed yet another test. And I feel like waving my good grades at the universe.

France, the one place in which my husband and I have attempted to live exclusively in a foreign language, is located in the mouth for me, as much for the rewards I garner when I speak as for the pleasures of its cuisine—including the horns of the warm, crisp-on-the-outside, soft-on-the-inside loaf of bread *à l'ancienne-nuh*— which does not make it to the picnic intact.

My husband and I, on a yearlong sabbatical some years ago, rented an apartment with few amenities in a little unglitzy beach town on the Côte d'Azur—an oxymoron, you might think, but they do exist: slightly tarnished and seedy-looking, like beach towns almost anywhere. This one was undistinguished enough to be frequented in the summer only by French folks from farther north. It was a town where no one we knew lived, not even the extraordinarily charming polyglot French anthropologist we met in Paris who encouraged us to go south and helped us find our place—his was about forty minutes away.

In the morning in the old-fashioned kitchen, with its stove and sink on legs, we tried to get the BBC on our shortwave radio. In that kitchen, I kept expecting to find a woman in a gingham apron with her hair in big loops behind each ear and puffed bangs over her forehead.

The fall light in the south of France—which is similar ecologically to Southern California, with its rocky, dry hills and opulent bougainvillea—seemed ratcheted down several notches from the light I was used to. Indeed, the apartment felt gray, gloomy, and chilly; I was unused to shuttered windows when I awoke, and I longed for full, flooding sunlight to bask in. The wind howled sometimes, echoing in the shafts of our apartment building. The combination of overcast skies and occasional surprisingly cold weather brought me back to my eastern U.S. childhood, with its fear of cold, its desire for the pleasure of warmth. And, inevitably, French was there every day with its foreignness: a small hill to climb, a detour to manage, a rut in the road to watch out for.

For, of course, suddenly living in exotic French was more dislocating than pleasant at first. My tongue flailed about in my mouth, like a person who can't find the right position for sleep. And it was difficult to settle into the idea of actually living and working at my projects in a place whose texture was not in my fingertips, the rhythm of whose weeks was not in my blood and which, therefore, could give no shape to my life. The strangeness at first refused to fade into the background. Small things distracted me: the light switch—annoyingly outside the room—that I couldn't flick on without thinking about it, as I would have at home. And yet, that dislocating strangeness, that suspension in time and space, is what one travels for; it gives us permission to not worry about our usual responsibilities, and to imagine change.

After a while, lonely, able to work only for a certain length of time each day, we gave ourselves over to the new slowness of our lives. We spent long afternoons wheeling our *chariot* around the Hypermarché Mammouth. The cheese counter stretched from here to gastronomic eternity, and each sample was more excruciatingly delicious than the last. As we told each other, the lamb tasted more lamby, the chicken more chickeny, than anything we'd ever hoped to experience; we needed only tiny portions to be fully satisfied. Lacking more technical vocabulary, we were too embarrassed to ask for rubbing alcohol (with the paints, it turned out), or which of the endless varieties of *crème fraîche* might approximate sour cream, or whether there was any margarine.

We took leisurely walks to the post office as I mentally rehearsed a little speech about rates and insurance for a present I had to mail home. I spent hours planning a phone conversation with a couple who had invited us to call (they'd offered their assistance in the *hypermarché*). Without visible gestures and facial expressions, making yourself understood in a language of which you have an uncertain command is that much harder.

I can't say exactly when those slow hours began to glow. But I know it had something to do with French itself. We had begun to accept and even enjoy the inevitable simplification that came with living in a new language, as well as the complications that resulted from failing to understand so much. And I can't say exactly when that glow heightened. Living in a foreign language is an automatic life-simplifier. It's as if in your own country you received a hundred channels, and suddenly, you have been reduced to just one or two. Street shouts, conversations in the department-store elevator, the buzz of TV—they can all be ignored, because they require an act of will to process. It is also disturbing at first, because your own cultural identity is shared only with the person you are with; only he or she knows who you are. You can be an island culture of two, surrounded by a sea of French, relying only on each other for the full range of human interaction that at home was spread among relatives, friends, colleagues. Ultimately we grew accustomed to the absence of stimuli, the phone that rarely rang, the lack of e-mail; we began to appreciate the possibility of hearing our own thoughts, and of seeing each other with new eyes.

But living in France, of course, invited venturing outside the isolation chamber and joining a community. And there, whatever else I was doing—debating between olives with fennel and olives with chili, or admiring the baby of the couple from the *hypermarché* (who were delighted we called and invited us to dinner)—I was also, in measured and tolerable doses, speaking French. And I was most pleasantly elevated to the post of number-one researcher, informant, and translator for my lavishly competent and knowledgeable—but not French-speaking—husband. Speaking French began to give my days enormous focus and a constant sense of accomplishment, as well as moments of utter annoyance—when, for example, my husband whispered loudly in my ear: "What is he saying? What? Tell him he's got it wrong . . ."

It was as if I had just one book to focus on, the book of French, which made me ignore a multitude of other books I might have leafed through. I thought of the ancients, who, before the proliferation of books, made one important text truly theirs by memorizing it, and then could endlessly refer to it, find everything they needed in it, locate themselves through it, even use it for divination and be comforted by it.

The words passing before my mind's eye—even the simplest of them, like *thé* for tea—with their rakish accents, their smart little hats, had a cachet that went with the pastel curls of ribbon on the white boxes from *la pâtisserie*, the white frills on the rack of lamb in the butcher shop, or the ceremony that accompanied the daily events of life, particularly the taking of meals.

Everything is aestheticized in France, especially women. Conversing in French, I felt as if I were contributing to that decorativeness. Could this have been because the French had successfully sold themselves to me as the epitome of chic, had successfully exported a glamorous view of their privileged selves from the time I first pasted a magazine picture of *la tour Eiffel* on my fourth-grade report cover? And because I was really a snob? This was the

European country that, sure enough, had sent the smallest group of immigrants to the United States. Oh, but it was good that they still pretended they hadn't learned any English, and still tried to legislate against their language being corrupted by *le weekend, le drugstore,* and the like. Thus, I could have the pleasure of eating goose liver *pâté* in a little restaurant where a chalkboard menu was briefly flashed at us as I savored the word, with its adorable little hat and feather at a jaunty angle, gliding along my mental blackboard, while my husband merely ate *patay.*

In the marriage-cocoon isolation chamber, I didn't feel the relentless aestheticizing as much as a young, unattached American computer artist working in Marseilles whom I met at a dinner hosted by the anthropologist. She was disgusted by the billboards of naked women that sell cars, *la maîtresse* on the side. As would be my own daughter, a year later, a student in a very touristy town. She would tell me that the young women she met at parties were too careful, afraid to enjoy themselves for fear of spoiling the tableaux they presented. I did notice a number of women pushing eighty who never let go, still wearing stiletto heels and stockings embroidered with decorations on the side as they clumped down streets where dog shit and perfume assaulted the nose with equal pungency.

But for us, there was only pleasure in the manners of France. Contrary to their press, we found the French almost ineluctably enchanting, polite, and imbued with an admirable sense of host-guest relations, though perhaps at times (we thought) masking some interior sadness. Theirs does seem to be a culture that values charisma over probity.

Charm oozed out of even the most modestly employed— teenage servers at McDonald's, for example. Could it be that because they were living in the known center of the universe they were spilling over with goodwill and desire to please? *"Monsieur? Madame?"* with the proper rising intonation rung out at the beginning and end of every conceivable transaction, even a no-sale. Even the dentist—whose bad root canal and crown cost me a molar— came personally to the waiting room to get me, bowed slightly in greeting, saw me to the door after my ordeal, and wished me a good weekend. During the visit, he had maintained his politeness until the seven-minute, technologically retro impression goo on the template between my locked jaws caused me to gag bigtime—at which point he got slightly hysterical.

But most of the time congeniality prevailed, and conversations with service-people and friends alike easily tracked the route of compliment. I glowed with the subtext (*vraiment, je parle français!*).

Another time, I had some troubling symptoms that resulted in a gynecological exam and, later, an ultrasound of my uterus. The gynecologist performed the ultrasound himself in his office. Doctors in France, greeted as Monsieur or Madame and not Docteur—just as they greet their patients—seem to be far less august and priestly figures than in the States, and have few technicians to do auxiliary work for them. This one was also remarkably handsome, which didn't help at all. As he moved the ultrasound wand across my plumpish belly, I was suddenly chagrined by my excessive flesh in the land of the genetically thin, and blurted out something about "*un peu grosse.*" "*Mais non,*" exclaimed Monsieur M., "*Pas du tout!*" and then something like "*C'est necessaire . . .*" or "*Il faut avoir . . . ,*" seeming to cross the doctor and suitor wires, which caused me to lose the remainder of his sentence and, blushing hotly, crawl inside my head in a paroxysm of embarrassment.

Was our delight simply the mirror of the Francophilia we projected, as we fell more in love with this savory and fragrant hiatus from our everyday lives and tensions? Where could one find someone so *aimable* as the man behind the counter at the little local market, who was always graciously willing to give a little disquisition on the flavors of, and best accompaniments for, his small selection of cheeses? Where could one find such delightful friends as the French family we fell into a dinner-and-outing schedule with, and whom we invited to meet our American friends when they passed through? With them we exchanged such lovely hostess gifts, such sincere oh-you-really-shouldn't-haves. But would we have enjoyed these acquaintances and friends so much if they didn't speak French? For me, speaking French was like an infusion of youth, as if, sure of the spotlight, I lived and at the same time watched myself living glamorously, as if in a movie.

Sometime after this sojourn, we returned to France, this time to Normandy, for a week. I had to take the language out of mothballs, air it out, try it on again. After a day or two and a few tastes of bread and cheese that reawakened taste buds I'd thought were forever dead, and a pleasant conversation with an *hôtelier* originally from the south, I began to find that place in my mouth and mind again, the pleasure of knowing the few subtleties I know: *baguette-tuh! fromage-zha!* But our visits are few and far between, and I am not a polyglot, so when I go again, I will undoubtedly once more be blissfully unable to forget that I am speaking French.

About the Contributors

Kate Adamek lives and writes in a cottage on Green Bay of Lake Michigan and works for the Red Cross. She has been a psychotherapist and social worker and has traveled abroad extensively, through countries including Nepal and India. She has lived in Vienna, Austria, Tanzania, and Turin, Italy.

Melinda Bergman Burgener was born in New York. She began writing after twenty years as a graphic designer, and her stories have appeared in magazines, newspapers, books, and on the web. She and her husband leave their San Francisco home each year to travel in France. She can be reached at WriteMelinda@mac.com.

About the Contributors

Valerie J. Brooks, a former fiction editor at *Northwest Review*, lives with her husband on the McKenzie River in Oregon. She has served on the board of directors for the Oregon Writers Colony and is co-coordinator of the Mid-Valley Willamette Writers Speakers Series. Her novel "Finding Vincible," currently with her agent, won the Monticello Award for fiction and earned her fellowships at Hedgebrook, Montalvo, and Vermont Studio Center. Her short story "Dead Children" appeared in the anthology *Scent of Cedars: Promising Writers of the Pacific Northwest*. She is currently working on a novel entitled "Stealing Paris."

M. F. K. Fisher, born Mary Frances Kennedy in 1908, grew up in Whittier, California. With her first husband, Alan Fisher, she lived in Dijon in the early 1930s. She wrote about those years in her memoir, *Long Ago in France* (from which her story is excerpted for this collection). Literary and opinionated, Fisher wrote more than two dozen books, including *Serve it Forth*, *How to Cook a Wolf*, *Gastronomical Me*, *The Art of Eating*, and *Two Towns in Provence*. Credited with creating the genre of food writing, Fisher was elected to the American Academy of Arts and Letters and received lifetime achievement awards from the James Beard Foundation and the American Institute of Wine and Food. She died in 1992.

Constance Hale loves the English language as much as she does the French, and has written two books on the subject, *Sin and Syntax: How to Craft Wickedly Effective Prose* and *Wired Style: Principles of English Usage in the Digital Age.* For her idiosyncratic approach she has been dubbed, by *Language International,* "Marion the Librarian on a Harley or E. B. White on acid." A former editor at the *San Francisco Examiner, Wired,* and *Health,* she has covered subjects ranging from national politics to Hawaiian culture for publications as diverse as *Honolulu,* the *Los Angeles Times,* the *Atlantic Monthly,* and *VIA* magazine.

Ayun Halliday is the author of *No Touch Monkey! And Other Travel Lessons Learned Too Late* and *The Big Rumpus: A Mother's Tale From the Trenches* and the creator/author of the zine *East Village Inky,* which won a 2002 Firecracker award. Her work has appeared in several anthologies, including *The Unsavvy Traveler: Women's Comic Tales of Catastrophe.* She is a contributing writer to *Utne, BUST,* and *Hip Mama.* She lives with her family in Brooklyn. Her book *Dilettante* will be published by Seal in spring 2005.

Georgia Hesse was the travel editor for the *San Francisco Sunday Examiner & Chronicle* for twenty years. She has written, cowritten, and contributed to books including travel guides to France and Paris (Fisher Travel Guides), *Voyages: The Romance of Cruising,* and *I Should Have Stayed Home: The Worst Trips of Great Writers.* Her work appears in publications such as *Country Living, Diversion, France Today, House Beautiful, Endless Vacation,* the *Los Angeles Times,* the *New York Post, VIA* magazine, and *Natural History.* She was awarded the Ordre du Mérite, given for her body of work on France, by the French government in 1982. In 1985, the Redwood Empire Association in Northern California instituted the Georgia Hesse Award for travel writing—Hesse was its first recipient. She lives in San Francisco and continues to write, teach, lecture, and travel.

Rikke Jorgensen is a San Francisco–based freelance writer whose work has appeared in *The Bark* magazine, the *San Francisco Chronicle*, the *Chicago Tribune*, the *Dallas Morning News*, the *Miami Herald*, and the *San Antonio Express-News*. She is an award-winning contributor to *Our Animals*, the San Francisco SPCA magazine, and her essays appear in a number of anthologies. She belongs to the rarest group of Francophile, the wine-indifferent.

Margaret Judge, a graduate of Illinois State University and a former teacher, lives in the San Francisco Bay Area with her husband. She is the author of the novel *Time and Time Again*.

Alice Kaplan was educated at Berkeley and Yale, and teaches French literature at Duke University. Her books include *French Lessons* (from which her story, "André," was excerpted for this collection), *Reproductions of Banality: Fascism, Literature, and French Intellectual Life.*

Judy Kronenfeld teaches in the creative writing department at the University of California, Riverside. Her essay, "Speaking French," appeared in a slightly different version in *Under the Sun.* Her fiction, creative nonfiction, reviews, and essays have appeared in publications including the *Madison Review*, the *North American Review*, *Potpourri*, the *Crescent Review*, the *AWP Chronicle*, *Chelsea*, and the *Literary Magazine Review*. Her poems have been published in magazines including *Hubbub*, *Poetry International*, *Passages North*, the *Chariton Review*, *Kansas Quarterly*, the *Manhattan Poetry Review*, the *Evansville Review*, the *Mississippi Valley Review*, and the *Women's Review of Books*.

Diane LeBow, based in San Francisco, has written stories for Salon.com, Travelers' Tales anthologies, *Erotic Travel Tales 2*, and numerous national newspapers and magazines. She travels the globe and has spent time with Afghan women, the Hopi, Amazon people, Tuvans, Mongolians, Corsicans, and Parisians. She has scuba-dived with sharks in the Red Sea and trained champion Morgan horses. A pioneer of college women's studies programs, she received her PhD in the history of consciousness from the University of California, began her teaching career in the Netherlands, and was a college professor for many years in Paris, New York City, and California. She is currently working on a book about her search for the best of all possible worlds.

Ericka Lutz lives in Oakland, California. Her fiction and creative nonfiction have appeared in numerous books, anthologies, and journals, including *Scrivener Creative Review*, *Side Show 1997: An Anthology of Contemporary Fiction*; *Child of Mine: Original Essays on Becoming a Mother*; *Toddler: Real-Life Stories of those Fickle, Irrational, Urgent, Tiny People We Love*; *Verve*; *Slate*; *Kaleidoscope*; and *Cherry Bleeds*. She is the author of seven commercial nonfiction books and the fiction editor at *Literary Mama*, and she teaches writing at University of California, Berkeley, and privately (www.erickalutz.com).

Lori Oliva lives and writes in Atlanta, Georgia. Her articles have appeared in national and regional business, health, and consumer publications. Currently, she is an editor for the national headquarters of Boys & Girls Clubs of America. She has also contributed to the Seal anthology *The Moment of Truth: Women's Funniest Romantic Catastrophes*.

Ginger Adams Otis lives in New York City. She writes for publications such as the *Village Voice, Ms., Newsday,* and *Jane* on such topics as the environment, human rights, women's issues, why people should sleep late, where to find good food, and her cat. She also travels around the globe on assignment for Lonely Planet.

Ruth Reichl, former restaurant critic of *New West* magazine, *California* magazine, the *Los Angeles Times,* and the *New York Times,* is the editor-in-chief of *Gourmet* magazine. She is the author of two book-length memoirs, *Tender at the Bone* (a James Beard Award finalist), and *Comfort Me with Apples* (from which her story in this collection was excerpted). Reichl lives in New York City with her husband and her son.

Susan Fox Rogers, based in New York, has edited ten book anthologies, including *Going Alone: Women's Adventures in the Wild*.

She is a recipient of a National Science Foundation award for writers and artists and teaches writing at Bard College.

Mary Schattenberg works as a healthcare consultant in Oakland, California, and is a freelance writer. She and her husband lived in Paris from 1997 to 1998, and return often. Her story "Beaujolais Nouveau" is part of a larger work in progress about living in France, written from a young hipster's point of view. She can be reached at maryschattenberg@yahoo.com.

Kay Sexton, a fiction writer who divides her time among France, the United Kingdom, and the United States, has an overdeveloped work ethic and a fig tree in her garden. She finds it hard to reconcile the two. She is a Jerry Jazz Musician New Short Fiction Award winner. Her website, www.charybdis.freeserve.co.uk, gives details of her current and forthcoming publications. Her love affair with France has been indiscriminate—her amours include Languedoc Roussillon, Paris, and the Ariège.

Dalia Sofer, a freelance writer living in New York, received her MFA from Sarah Lawrence College and has contributed regularly to publications including *Poets & Writers* magazine, the *American Journal of Nursing,* and the *New York Sun.* Her 2001 essay "Of These, Solitude," appeared in the anthology *Yentl's Revenge: The Next Wave of Jewish Feminism.* She is currently working on a novel about a man imprisoned in Iran following the 1979 revolution.

Lisa Solod, who recently returned from two years in Paris, has written for the *International Herald Tribune* as well as many other newspapers and magazines. Her work has appeared in numerous literary publications and anthologies, including *An Inn Near Kyoto: Writing by American Women Abroad,* and she has received a number of fellowships to the Virginia Center for the Creative Arts.

Susan M. Tiberghien, an American living in Switzerland, has published two memoirs, *Looking for Gold: A Year in Jungian Analysis* and *Circling to the Center: One Woman's Encounter with Silent Prayer,* a forthcoming collection of essays, *Footstep: A European Album;* and shorter work in journals and anthologies. She teaches writing workshops for the International Women's Writing Guild, for C.G. Jung Centers, and for the Geneva Writers' Group, where she edits the review *Offshoots: Writing from Geneva.*

Alice B. Toklas was born Alice Babette Toklas in San Francisco in 1877. In 1907 she moved to France where she and her lifelong companion, Gertrude Stein, presided over their famous literary salon on 27, rue de Fleurus in Paris. Their salon was frequented by Ernest Hemingway, F. Scott Fitzgerald, Sherwood Anderson, Matisse, Picasso, Gris, and Braque, to name just a few of its many luminaries. The now classic *Alice B. Toklas Cook Book* (from which her story is excerpted for this anthology) was first published in 1954 and is as much memoir as cookbook of the culinary adventures of Stein and

Toklas in Paris and throughout France. Toklas died in 1967, twenty years after Stein's death.

Monique Y. Wells has written for the *International Herald Tribune*, the *San Francisco Chronicle*, the *Los Angeles Times*, *This City Paris*, *France Today*, and *Upscale*. She is the author of *Food for the Soul: A Texas Expatriate Nurtures Her Culinary Roots in Paris*; co-author of *Paris Reflections: Walks through African-American Paris* and Christiann Anderson; and co-owner of Discover Paris!, personalized itineraries for independent travelers (www.discoverparis.net).

About the Editor

Camille Cusumano, currently an editor at *VIA* magazine in San Francisco, began her professional life in the French press, at *Le Journal Français*. She has contributed to two other Seal anthologies (*Women Who Eat: A New Generation on the Glory of Food* and *Far From Home: Father-Daughter Travel Adventures*). Her short story, "A dying tiger moaned for drink," was a finalist for the 2003 Katherine Anne Porter Prize for fiction. She has written for publications including the *New York Times*, the *Los Angeles Times*, the *San Francisco Chronicle*, *Islands*, and *Country Living*. She is the author of several cookbooks and a novel, *The Last Cannoli*, a finalist for the 2000 James Jones First Novel Fellowship.

Selected Titles from Seal Press

No Touch Monkey! And Other Travel Lessons Learned Too Late by Ayun Halliday. $14.95. 1-58005-097-2. A self-admittedly bumbling vacationer, Halliday shares—with razor-sharp wit and to hilarious effect—the travel stories most are too self-conscious to tell.

Give Me the World by Leila Hadley. $14.95, 1-58005-091-3. The spirited story of one young woman's travels by boat and by land with her six-year-old son.

No Hurry to Get Home: The Memoir of the New Yorker Writer Whose Unconventional Life and Adventures Spanned the Twentieth Century by Emily Hahn. $14.95, 1-58005-045-X. Hahn's memoir captures her free-spirited, charismatic personality and her inextinguishable passion for the unconventional life.

The Unsavvy Traveler: Women's Comic Tales of Catastrophe edited by Rosemary Caperton, Anne Mathews, and Lucie Ocenas. $15.95, 1-58005-058-1. Twenty-five gut-wrenchingly funny responses to the question: What happens when trips go wrong?

A Woman Alone: Travel Tales from Around the Globe edited by Faith Conlon, Ingrid Emerick, and Christina Henry de Tessan. $15.95, 1-58005-059-X. A collection of rousing stories by women who travel solo.

East Toward Dawn: A Woman's Solo Journey Around the World by Nan Watkins. $14.95, 1-58005-064-6. After the loss of her son and the end of a marriage, the author sets out in search of joy and renewal in travel.

Gift of the Wild: A Woman's Book of Adventure edited by Faith Conlon, Ingrid Emerick, and Jennie Goode. $16.95, 1-58005-006-9. Explores the transformative power of outdoor adventure in the lives of women.

Seal Press publishes many outdoors and travel books by women writers. Please visit our website at www.sealpress.com.